SO-BCY-287

ALL YOU NEED TO KNOW ABOUT
SOLITAIRE FROM THE EXPERTS!

ALBERT H. MOREHEAD, known as the "modern Hoyle," was the former Games Editor of The New York Times, and author of the world famous CONTRACT BRIDGE SUMMARY, plus 50 other books on card games.

GEOFFREY MOTT-SMITH, an authority on the philosophy, strategy and mathematics of games, was the former editor of Games Digest and The Bridge World.

Bantam Game and Puzzle Books
Ask your bookseller for the books you have missed

THE BACKGAMMON BOOK by Oswald Jacoby and John R. Crawford
THE BANTAM CROSSWORD PUZZLE BOOK #2 by J. L. Wilkinson
THE BANTAM CROSSWORD PUZZLE BOOK #3 by J. L. Wilkinson
THE BANTAM CROSSWORD PUZZLE BOOK #4 by Jack Luzzatto
THE BANTAM CROSSWORD PUZZLE BOOK #5 by Jack Luzzatto
THE BANTAM CROSSWORD PUZZLE BOOK #7 by Jack Luzzatto
THE BANTAM CROSSWORD PUZZLE BOOK #11 by Jack Luzzatto
BANTAM ONE A DAY CROSSWORDS #2 by Edward Julius
BANTAM ONE A DAY CROSSWORDS #3 by Edward Julius
BANTAM ONE A DAY CROSSWORDS #4 by Edward Julius
THE BANTAM TRIVIA QUIZ BOOK #1 by Donald Saltz
THE BANTAM TRIVIA QUIZ BOOK #2 by Donald Saltz
BOBBY FISCHER TEACHES CHESS by Bobby Fischer, Stuart Margulies and
  Donn Mosenfelder
THE COMPLETE BOOK OF SOLITAIRE AND PATIENCE GAMES by Albert H.
  Moorehead and Geoffrey Mott-Smith
THE DOMINO BOOK by Fredrick Berndt
FISCHER-SPASSKY: THE NEW YORK TIMES REPORT ON THE CHESS MATCH
  OF THE CENTURY by Richard Roberts with Harold C. Schonberg, Al
  Horowitz and Samuel Reshevsky
GAMESMAN BRIDGE by Edwin Kantar and Jackson Stanley
HIDE AND SEEK WORD PUZZLES #1 by Jack Looney
HIDE AND SEEK WORD PUZZLES #2 by Peter Tasler and Jack Dean
HIDE AND SEEK WORD PUZZLES #3 by Jack Looney
HOW TO BEAT BOBBY FISCHER by Edmar Mednis
PEOPLES BICENTENNIAL COMMISSION QUIZ BOOK OF THE AMERICAN
  REVOLUTION
HOW TO PLAY WINNING CHESS by Fred Reinfeld
THE ROGER CARAS NATURE QUIZ BOOK #1 by Roger Caras
THE ROGER CARAS NATURE QUIZ BOOK #2 by Roger Caras
A SHORT CUT TO WINNING BRIDGE by Alfred Sheinwold
WINNING CONTRACT BRIDGE COMPLETE by Edgar Kaplan
WORD + CROSS by Sam Saxon

THE COMPLETE BOOK OF
SOLITAIRE AND
PATIENCE GAMES

By ALBERT H. MOREHEAD
and GEOFFREY MOTT-SMITH

*This low-priced Bantam Book
has been completely reset in a type face
designed for easy reading, and was printed
from new plates. It contains the complete
text of the original hard-cover edition.*
NOT ONE WORD HAS BEEN OMITTED.

THE COMPLETE BOOK OF SOLITAIRE AND PATIENCE GAMES
*A Bantam Book / published by arrangement with
David McKay Company, Inc.*

PRINTING HISTORY
*Longman's Green ediiton published 1949
Grosset & Dunlap edition published July 1953
Bantam edition / December 1966*

2nd printing	*February 1967*	*7th printing ....*	*May 1976*
3rd printing	*October 1968*	*8th printing ....*	*June 1977*
4th printing	*August 1973*	*9th printing ....*	*June 1978*
5th printing	*February 1974*	*10th printing ......*	*August 1979*
6th printing	*February 1975*	*11th printing ....*	*July 1980*

Contents

Index to Games

About Solitaire Games—and About This Book

I

It is natural to suppose that solitaire games preceded card games for two or more players. We can easily imagine how solitaire grew out of the rites of dealing and selection, the pictorial layouts, of fortune-telling, and divination is the first known use of the *tarots*.

Alas! this is conjecture. The historical record, none too certain in respect to games and sports generally, is particularly wanting as to solitaire.

The ultimate origin of playing cards is a matter of scholarly dispute. But it is agreed that they were introduced to northern Europe, probably from Italy, during the fourteenth century. We even know the principal rules of a game played at that time, *tarocchini* or *tarok*. (It survives to this day in central Europe.) But not until the nineteenth century, it seems, did anyone trouble to record the rules of a solitaire game for posterity.

A news letter dated 1816 reports that Napoleon Bonaparte, in exile at St. Helena, occupies his time in "playing patience." This is the earliest reference to patience as a game unearthed by the Oxford English Dictionary. It is evident that "patience" was no neologism, but on the contrary, was in such familiar usage as to require no elucidation.

We ourselves have found a reference to the playing of patience in Tolstoy's *War and Peace*, in a scene supposed to have taken place in 1808. We believe that Tolstoy was most careful in historical allusions; this reference can the more readily be accepted as not anachronistic since Tolstoy was himself a passionate devotee of solitaire.

There are probably much earlier references in French literature. The earliest English books on patience appear to have drawn on French sources; the very names of the games are almost all French—La Belle Lucie, Les Quatre Coins, L'Horloge, La Nivernaise, La Loi Salique, Le Carré Napoléon, etc.

II

Whether Napoleon invented any of the games bearing his name, or even whether he played them, we do not know. Perhaps they were older games, renamed for the First Consul by his admirers. During his brilliant military campaigns in Italy and Austria, thousands of commercial products changed to the brand "Napoleon." Alternatively, it is possible that the Napoleon solitaires were invented during the extraordinarily fecund period of the Revolution (from 1789 to about 1800). This was the heyday of experiments and innovations in playing cards. It was at this time that the ace (taken to symbolize the lowest social class) began to be regularly placed above the king (the nobility). Old designs gave way to new symbols of the Revolution. At some gambling casinos the faces of the cards changed daily, and the "house rule" as to the ranking of the cards changed three times in a week.

Many new games, and new variants of old games, were invented during this period. It is natural to suppose that the solitaire family also effloresced. But again history failed to supply a chronicler.

There is no reference to solitaire, much less the description of a particular reference, in the books on which we rely for the early history of card games—such as Charles Cotton's *The Compleat Gamester* (1674), Abbé Bellecour's *Academie des jeux* (1768), *Bohn's Handbook of Games* (1850).

III

The first compendium of solitaire games in English was, we believe, Lady Adelaide Cadogan's *Illustrated Games of Patience*, about 1870. This pioneer work ran through many editions and even today is occasionally reprinted. In England, it has made the name "Cadogan" to some degree a common noun, meaning any book on solitaire, much as any book on card games in general is called a "Hoyle."

Spurred no doubt by Lady Cadogan's example, two other ladies hastened to repair the hiatus in games literature, Mrs. E. D. Cheney with *Patience* and Annie B. Henshaw with *Amusements for Invalids* (Boston, 1870). Soon the publishers of handbooks on chess, whist, croquet, badminton and the like added solitaire to their lists. In 1883 Dick & Fitzgerald of New York issued their first series of *Dick's Games of Pa-*

PRINTERS INK
Scottsdale Mall
South Bend, Ind.
2

- 5 JUN 81

＄001.70   3

＄000.07   X

1398   ＄001.77   BAL
                   DUE   —

tience, following with a second series in 1898. These excellently printed and illustrated volumes greatly extended the list of recorded solitaires.

By the end of the century, there was no dearth of books on solitaire. Among others who made notable contributions were "Cavendish" (H. E. Jones), "Professor Hoffmann" (Angelo Lewis), Basil Dalton, and Ernest Bergholt.

IV

Solitaire is traditionally a game for invalids, shut-ins, recluses. By a quirk of fate (or man), those who have the greatest use for playing cards are denied them. American prisons and asylums class playing cards as lethal weapons—because they are edged! The inmates must forego cards, or use the substitutes sometimes provided—thick tiles bearing the impress of playing-card designs. The more elaborate solitaires, we are told, are attempted only by "lifers."

At least one shut-in has surmounted the difficulties. The late Bill Beers was an inmate of a mental asylum. He invented not only a great many worthwhile chess problems but also the excellent patience which we herein list as Cribbage Solitaire III. We suggest "Bill Beers" as an appropriate variant name.

The following passage occurs in Somerset Maugham's *The Gentleman in the Parlour:*

"I reproached myself as I set out the cards. Considering the shortness of life and the infinite number of important things there are to do during its course, it can only be the proof of a flippant disposition that one should waste one's time in such a pursuit . . . But I knew seventeen varieties of patience. I tried the spider and never by any chance got it out . . ."

One wonders whether this self-reproach was sincere. It is not "proof of a flippant disposition" to take recreation. We are reminded of a man in real life, a statesman who bore no inconsiderable burden of responsibility; at moments of crisis, when he could but wait the outcome of events, he was wont to relax with solitaire. Oddly enough, he too was a devotee of Spider. His name was Franklin Delano Roosevelt.

The catharsis of patience has been recognized by many novelists. We have mentioned Tolstoy, who himself had an addiction to patience bordering on superstition. At times of perplexity, he played cards to decide his course (though he has confessed that when he disliked the answer he shuffled the cards and dealt anew). In Dostoevsky's *The Brothers Karamazov* the character Grushenka resorts to solitaire to weather an almost unbearable period of suspense. (The game is called "Fools," which may be a Russian equivalent of the English pejorative "Idiot's Delight.")

V

Another name that has become almost a common noun is "Canfield."

Mr. Canfield was the proprietor of a fashionable gambling salon at Saratoga in the Gay Nineties. His proposition was: you purchase a deck for fifty dollars and play a game of the solitaire Canfield; I will pay you five dollars for every card in your foundation piles when the game is over. According to R. F. Foster, the player's average expectation is between five and six cards, so that Mr. Canfield stood to win about twenty-five dollars per game. Despite this inordinate "house percentage," his proposition was accepted by thousands, and the cult of Canfield spread all over the country. Mr. Canfield is supposed to have garnered a fortune, but he later stated that his solitaire room was less lucrative than the roulette wheel. Two housemen operating the wheel could handle a score of customers, whereas for every solitaire punter he had to hire a houseman to watch the player for fraud.

The game actually played at Canfield's Casino is that described as "Canfield." But the name has been very widely misapplied to another game, Klondike, which is by far the most-played solitaire today.

However, the time has come when we may well cease insisting that Canfield is a misnomer for Klondike. "Canfield" has become almost a generic name for patience itself.

During WPA days, a subsidized citizen submitted to our editorial eye a manuscript entitled "Chances of Winning at Solitaire." The attack on this knotty problem was purely empirical; the industrious author had played over 5,000 games and recorded the results of each. Internal evidence indicated that the 5,000 trials were all upon the same solitaire—but *what* solitaire was nowhere divulged. Inquiry elicited the fact that the author thought "Solitaire" to be the name of a specific game—the only one known to him. When we asked its rules, he complied with a description of Klondike.

This incident is but one of many that have convinced us

(a) Klondike is the only solitaire known to thousands of benighted persons; (b) all but a few bibliophiles like ourselves call it Canfield or simply Solitaire.

How Klondike came to be selected as the popular favorite is an inexplicable mystery. One would think, *a priori*, that it is among the least likely candidates for supremacy. One would expect the mantle to fall on a solitaire that can be won frequently, or that gives great scope for skill, or that requires little time to play. Klondike fails in all three respects. The player's chance of winning is surely not greater than 1 in 30; the few choices that arise must be settled by guesswork; a game takes more than the average time for one-deck solitaires.

It may well be that the vogue of Klondike is on the wane. Reaction against its difficulty has produced one of the *curiosa* of games—a way of stacking a deck so as to win Klondike. Proceed as follows:

Arrange each suit in order, king to ace, from the top of the deck down, suits alternating in color (as, spades, hearts, clubs, diamonds). Deal the deck into four piles, one card at a time, face down. Then gather the piles, each on the pile to its right, so that the first-dealt will be at the top of the new stock.

Now play a game of Klondike, being careful not to disarrange the stacked deck. Deal the layout by rows. Make every possible play, every possible space, with these exceptions:

Do not play any additional cards upon the aces until you have turned the last card of the stock. (Some cards could be played up earlier, but this rule simplifies the game.)

Early in the game the only choice arises: two sixes are available for build on a seven. Choose the six from the larger pile, at the extreme right. (The game can be won after play of the other six, but only with some extra precautions.)

VI

It may be asked why, if the literature of solitaire is now so extensive, we have the temerity to offer yet another book.

We believe that this book offers the following distinctive features:

1. Description of more than 150 solitaires, including all of the best and most-played.

The size of this list is made possible in part by the condensation of description. But we have not had to omit any essential rule, nor resort to such extremes of formalization as are found in other books with a less generous allotment of pages.

In order to make a representative selection, we first listed and compared every game and every variant known to us, through books and other sources. We made a classification of types, and have included at least one example of each category. In some categories there are so many examples, differing only in trifles, that we eliminated about a hundred oft-described but little-played games, such as Zodiac, Hemispheres, Light and Shade, The Gathering of the Clans. On the other hand, certain categories were empty; certain interesting ideas have been exploited little or not at all. To fill the void we have invented a number of new games, here described for the first time: Boomerang, Bristol, Dutchess, Fission, Glencoe, Moojub, Stalactites, Strategy, Sudden Death, Xerxes, and Zingara.

2. Advice on skillful play, where opportunities for skill exist.

Not a few are attracted to solitaire as a battle of wits against chance. Our "tips" do not undertake to provide a formula for winning, but to draw attention to the ways in which the player can control the outcome.

3. Checking of all contingencies that arise in solitaire play to assure that each is adequately covered by the rules.

We are convinced that few of the compilers of the past have actually played more than a dozen of the games they have described. We played every game in our file—about four hundred, including variants. We speedily discovered that many were unplayable under extant rules—situations would frequently arise of which the rules said nothing. By research in earlier sources we recovered some of the missing rules (later copyists having made slips of omission). In other cases, we supplied rules upon our own experience.

4. Supplying of variants for games that are, under traditional rules, excessively difficult or excessively easy.

We believe that a solitaire extreme in either direction will be played at all only if it has a feature of striking interest. By this criterion we have eliminated some time-honored but "impossible" or "self-working" games. Any that are, to our knowledge, much played, have been therefor retained. Examples are Royal Parade and Nivernaise. These games allow for choices that ought to make them games of skill, but the long odds against winning nullify the benefits of the choice. We have therefore devised the variants Virginia Reel and Tournament, which we immodestly rate in the top bracket for skill. (Both of these variants have been described in *Games Digest*, during 1938.)

For the difficult Spiderette, we have supplied a variant that offers more reasonable odds, Will o' the Wisp.

New also is Selective Canfield, which gives somewhat improved chances against the "Demon." We believe we are the first to introduce the joker into solitaire, in our Joker Canfield and Joker Klondike. Our suggestion of scoring degrees of victory, as in Par Pyramid and Tournament Golf, may well be applied to other low-chance games.

5. Listing of many variant names for the same game.

The object is to increase the utility of the book. You may know your favorite solitaire by some name other than that most widely used.

We have exercised considerable editorial license in the selection of primary names, chiefly to avoid ambiguity. "Idiot's Delight" is relegated to a variant name; it has been applied to so many different games as to have become a kind of synonym for "solitaire." "Thirteens" is once-used as a primary name, to accord with kindred "Tens," "Fourteens," etc., but everywhere else is relegated to a variant name. We have rechristened one of the "Perpetual Motions" as "Rondo" and one of the "Clocks" as "Big Ben." To supply the want of a distinctive primary name we have devised "Gargantua," "Osmosis," "Easthaven," and "Laggard Lady."

The names "Spiderette" and "Scorpion" for well-known games were proposed by us in articles published some years ago, the idea being to mark the "arachnid" relationship to Spider. It is too bad that "Little Spider" is traditionally so called, for it belongs to an entirely different family from (Big) Spider. In this case, as with Napoleon at St. Helena and St. Helena, we have felt that the old names are too well-established to be shelved.

The Little Corporal is memorialized in several solitaires, notably Napoleon at St. Helena, Napoleon's Square, and Napoleon's Favorite. In casual parlance all these names tend to degenerate to "Napoleon" and so become indistinguishable. The ambiguity between the first two is not serious. As pointed out by Cavendish, Le Carré Napoléon (Napoleon's Square) is the same as the other, the tableau piles being arranged in a square instead of a row. But the third game is different, and whether you call it Napoleon's Favorite or St. Heléna there is ambiguity with Napoleon at St. Helena. This is the one instance in which we have felt that the traditional names should be preserved (as our "trunk names" rather than as "variants") even at the cost of ambiguity.

6. **Estimate of the time required to play, and the chances of winning, each game.**

We hasten to state that we have *not* determined the chances by playing 5,000 games of each solitaire.

We have simply made a guess at what such a test would show, on the basis of data admittedly insufficient for scientific precision. Possibly some figures are wide of the mark. We shall expect to receive irate letters from some readers, taking us to task. We are inured to that sort of thing. Some years ago, in writing of Accordion, we stated that we had never heard of anyone winning it. Immediately we received a (relative) deluge of letters (seven), saying typically: "I have played Accordion every night for twenty years, and I have won it no less than three times."

We still hold that certain games are, for practical purposes, "impossible." To the few included in this book we have given the rating 1/100, but the actual odds may be more nearly 1/10,000.

The shortest odds we give are 9/10; some of the games so rated may actually be sure-things against any fall of the cards. But near-certainty does not mean that a game is self-working. On the contrary, most of these are games with very great opportunity for skill; you can win almost every time, but you have to work for it.

One objective kept in mind in selecting the games was to cover the gamut from 9/10 to 1/100. The reader seeking a new pastime can find an assortment of solitaires offering about the degree of difficulty he prefers.

VII

This book condenses the description of each game by relying on certain specially-defined terms. Before turning to the games, read the preface "General Procedure of Solitaire" and become acquainted with the terminology.

The games are grouped in three sections, according to the number of decks used: (a) one deck; (b) two decks; (c) others—one, two, and four stripped decks, four complete decks. The last section includes a description of Russian Bank. Though not strictly a solitaire, but a two-handed game, Russian Bank is played in the manner of a solitaire, with foundations, tableau, reserve, stock, and wastepile.

To locate a specific game known to you by name, look in the alphabetical index in the front of the book. If you do not find it listed, perhaps it is described under a different name. Browse through the appropriate section and look at the diagrams—perhaps you will recognize your quarry. Within each section, similar games are grouped together, so far as is practicable. Thus, to find any variant of Canfield, Klondike, Napoleon at St. Helena, etc., look in the pages immediately following these games.

ALBERT H. MOREHEAD

GEOFFREY MOTT-SMITH

How to Choose a Solitaire Game

Solitaires differ widely in the opportunities they afford for the exercise of skill. Some, like Block Eleven, are purely mechanical. Others, like Sly Fox, can probably be won against any fall of the cards, by the exercise of sufficient patience and foresight. Many, like Calculation, call for utmost skill but often nullify it through bad luck.

It is no slur upon a solitaire to say that it is purely mechanical or gives little scope for skill. Indeed, the games of this type are the most restful. But IF you wish to pit your wits against the luck of the deal, IF you wish to bedevil your brain with tortuous calculation, here is a list for your guidance.

The following lists of "Solitaires of Skill" represent, of course, the personal opinion of the authors. But due attention has been given to certain objective criteria. To give scope for skill, a game must give choices of play in reasonable number and frequency. Furthermore, these choices must have discernible effect on the outcome. No game that has a slight chance of being won—say worse than one chance in ten— can be a game of skill, because the choices palpably do not have sufficient effect on the outcome.

The games are listed alphabetically; we do not undertake to determine an individual ranking.

Solitaires giving maximum opportunity for skill

ONE DECK
  Baker's Dozen
  Beleaguered Castle
  Bristol
  Calculation
  Eight Off
  Fission
  Flower Garden

  Good Measure
  La Belle Lucie
  Little Spider
  Poker Patience
  Shamrocks
  Strategy
  Trefoil
  Yukon

TWO DECKS
Big Ben
British Square
Constitution
Corner Stones
Crazy Quilt
Crescent
Frog
Gavotte
House on the Hill
House in the Wood
Intelligence

Maria
Sly Fox
Spider
Terrace
Tournament
Virginia Reel

OTHER
Boomerang
Olga
Sudden Death

Solitaires giving moderate opportunity for skill

ONE DECK
Bisley
Chessboard
Cribbage Patience III
Fortress
Grandfather's Clock
Pendulum
Puss in Corner
Stalactites
Suspense
Tournament Golf
Whitehead
Will o' the Wisp

TWO DECKS
Alhambra
Capricieuse
Colorado
Diplomat
Four Intruders
Napoleon at St. Helena
Parallels
Royal Cotillion
Salic Law
St. Helena
Triumph
Windmill

FOUR DECKS
Empress of India

General Procedure of Solitaire

(With explanation of terms)

Cards. All solitaires are based on the standard deck of 52 cards. Most solitaires use either one deck, or two decks shuffled together. Some few use more than two decks; a few others use one deck reduced to 40, 32, or 20 cards, or the Pinochle deck, which is actually two decks stripped to the nines.

This book introduces for the first time solitaire games using the joker, a fifty-third card added to the standard deck.

Playing cards are made in two principal sizes: 2½ inches wide and 2¼ inches wide (the length being 3½ inches in each case). The narrower size is recommended for all solitaires, to save room in the layout. Decks are manufactured in miniature sizes, 2 to 2¾ inches in length. A miniature deck, if you can handle it (shuffling is more difficult) is a convenience for the many solitaires with large layouts.

Important to nearly all solitaires is that the deck be very thoroughly shuffled before dealing begins.

Suits and sequence. The standard deck comprises 13 cards each of four suits: spades (♠), hearts (♡), diamonds (◇), clubs (♣).

The cards in each suit are: A, 2, 3, 4, 5, 6, 7, 8, 9, 10, J, Q, K. This order is the basic rank from low (ace) to high (king). In many cases the ranking is *continuous*, that is, the ace is in sequence above the king as well as below the two. In a few cases the sequence has top and bottom limits other than king and ace. All such variations from the basic sequence are remarked in the text of this book.

When the cards are considered as numerical quantities, the king is 13, the queen 12, the jack 11, the ace 1.

Layout. Many solitaires commence with the dealing of a fixed number of cards upon the table, in some conventional pattern. The totality of all cards so dealt is called the *layout*.

Where any cards of the layout are dealt face down, the

fact is noted in this book. In the absence of such note, deal all cards face up.

Patterns commonly encountered in the layout are "rows" and "columns," which may or may not be "overlapped"; also "piles" and "fans." For convenience of reference, certain groups of cards in the layout may be designated as "foundations," "tableau," "reserve," or by descriptive terms such as "wing." Particularized terms are explained when they occur; the general terms are defined and illustrated on the following pages.

Row—a line of cards parallel to the edge of the table at which the player is seated.

A row is dealt from left to right. If it is *overlapped,* each card is laid upon that previously dealt, so as to cover most of its face but leave the index in the upper left corner visible. The "top card" or "right end" of an overlapped row is the card that would be uppermost if the row were shoved together into a pile.

Column—a line of cards perpendicular to the edge of the table at which the player is seated.

A column is dealt from the point farthest from the player, toward himself. The far point is the *top,* being nearest the top of the page in a diagram; the card nearest the player is at the bottom of the diagram and is referred to as the "bottom card."

If the cards in a column are *overlapped,* each card is laid upon that previously dealt so as to cover most of its face but leave the index in the upper left corner visible. To avoid ambiguity as to which is then the "bottom" card, a column of overlapping cards is referred to, in this book, as a *spread pile* or a *pile spread downward;* and the top card of the pile is that card which is not covered in whole or in part by any other.

Pile—a batch of cards dealt upon each other and squared up in a compact heap.

A series of piles is often dealt by laying out a row or column, then another row or column on top of the first, and so on.

The object in making a pile, instead of overlapping the cards, may be either (a) to save room, or (b) to prevent more than one card at a time from being visible. In case (b),

ELEMENTS OF THE LAYOUT

Row of cards

COLUMN

Overlapping row

top of fan

Fan

a card dealt face up

place reserved for a card to come

a card face down

Pile, squared up

top of pile

bottom of column

Pile, spread downward

Spread Piles, dealt by rows

the pile should usually be dealt face down, then squared and turned face up. In the absence of a specific rule to the contrary, any pile of face-up cards may be spread for inspection of lower cards.

The top card of a pile is that card which is not covered by any other.

Fan—an overlapped row, usually made by counting the cards off the deck face down, then spreading them face up with a sweep of the hand.

Foundations—the first cards of certain piles, where the object of play is to build the entire deck upon these piles.

Most solitaires—though not all—use foundations. When the foundations are part of the layout, you are directed to "Remove (certain cards) from the deck and put them in a (row or column)." When the foundations are not part of the layout, you are directed to "Move (certain cards), as they become available, to a (row or column)."

The foundations are usually all the cards of a specified rank (often, aces). Sometimes the rank is fixed by chance in the deal; in a few cases, the foundations are cards of different ranks.

Whenever foundations are used, assume the following rules to hold unless exceptions are specifically noted:

1. A card once built on a foundation may not be moved elsewhere.

2. A foundation card may not be built upon until it is in the foundation row; usually it must be moved to the foundation row as soon as it becomes available (unless it was prefixed there).

3. Building in other parts of the layout stops at the rank next to the foundation cards. For example, if aces are foundations, and there is building downward in the tableau, nothing may be built on a two and a king may not be built on any other card.

4. When the foundation is other than ace or king, these two cards are in sequence. For example, if sevens are foundations, the sequence of rank is: 7 (low), 8, 9, 10, J, Q, K, A, 2, 3, 4, 5, 6 (high).

Winning a game. At this juncture we may well explain what is meant by "winning" a solitaire game.

Whenever foundations are used the object of play is to build the entire deck upon them, and the game is won if this object is achieved.

When there are no foundations, the objective that constitutes winning is stated specifically.

Whether "partial winning" exists is a subjective matter. If you play Canfield for recreation, you may consider that you have lost if you do not "get out" all fifty-two cards; but had you played for stakes against Mr. Canfield you would have been happy—and a winner—to get out eleven or more cards. In the case of some of the long-chance solitaires, this book gives scoring methods that allow for degrees of victory.

Reserve, Tableau. These terms designate parts of the layout other than foundations. Rigid definition would impair their usefulness. But on a *reserve* no building is ever allowed; on a *tableau* building is usually allowed, though not invariably.

Spaces. Wherever a reserve or tableau comprises separate cards, piles, or overlapped rows, the removal entire of any such unit (including any cards built upon it) leaves a *space*. The rules of each game state whether and how a space may be filled. In many cases, the chief opportunity for skill is afforded by the utilization of spaces.

Stock—the remainder of the deck, after the layout is dealt. The stock must always be kept in a pile, face down.

The stock is brought into play in either of two ways: (a) cards are turned up from it one at a time, each becoming available for building as it is turned up; (b) cards are dealt into spaces, or dealt upon the original layout in added batches.

Wastepile. When cards from the stock may be added to the layout only under certain restrictions as to building, the unplayable cards are laid face up in one or more *wastepiles*. Cards placed in a wastepile may be brought back into play later; usually, the top card of a wastepile is available for play.

Building—placing one card upon another in the foundations or tableau, under certain restrictions.

Any of the following rules may apply as to suit:

1. *Regardless of suit.* (Building is governed by rank alone; as, any seven may be built on any eight.)

2. *In suit*. (As, a spade only on another spade; with due attention, of course, to any rules as to the rank of the cards.)

3. *In color*. (A black card only on another black card, a red card only on another red card; as, a spade on either a spade or a club.)

4. *In alternate colors*. (A black card only on a red, a red only on a black.)

5. *On any suit but its own*. (As, a spade on a heart, diamond, or club but not on another spade.)

Any of the following rules may apply as to rank:

1. *Up*. (A card on a next-lower card. Thus, "building up in suit" means that a $\diamondsuit$ 10 goes on a $\diamondsuit$ 9, etc. "Building up regardless of suit" means that any ten goes on any nine.)

2. *Down*. (A card on a next-higher card. Thus, "building down in alternate colors" means that a $\heartsuit$ 7 goes on either a $\spadesuit$ 8 or a $\clubsuit$ 8.)

3. *Up*, or *down, by* (*a given interval*). (For example, building up *by twos* means that a three may be built on an ace, a five on a three, etc., giving the full sequence A, 3, 5, 7, 9, J, K, 2, 4, 6, 8, 10, Q. In every case the text states or illustrates the permissible sequence.)

4. *Either up or down*. (A nine either on a ten or on an eight, subject to any restriction as to suit. Sometimes the direction of building may be reversed at will, sometimes, once begun, it may not be changed; the rule applying to the game in question is always stated in the text.)

Build—two or more cards on top of a pile, conforming in suit and sequence to the rules for building on that pile. Usually, where it is permissible to move a build as a single unit, the entire build must be moved, not a portion of it. Sometimes either the top card or the entire build may be moved. When a build is moved as a unit, it is the bottommost card of the build that must fit the card to which the build is moved.

Available card—one that may under the rules be moved elsewhere.

In the absence of any rule to the contrary, assume that the available cards are: Any card of tableau or reserve not covered in whole or in part by another; the top card of each wastepile; a card newly turned from the stock.

A rule that "the top of a pile," "the bottom of a column,"

etc., is available, means that the removal of such card makes the next one to it available.

Discard—to lay a card aside, out of play for the rest of the game.

Some few games use a "cut" or "stripped" deck—one from which certain cards are discarded before dealing begins.

In some full-deck games, cards are discarded during the course of the play. In this event, the object of play is usually to discard all or most of the deck; such games do not usually use foundations.

Redeal. Wherever the stock is brought into play one card at a time, unplayable cards being laid in one or more wastepiles, the permission to *redeal* applies only to the wastepiles. That is, the cards of all wastepiles are gathered in a heap and turned face down, forming a new stock which is then turned up one card at a time as before. "Two redeals are allowed" means that the stock may be run through three times in all, and so on.

In some cases the stock is run through in batches of three, and in all such cases at least two redeals are allowed—the stock may be run through three times. In some cases, the stock may be run through time after time without limit, until the game is made or blocked.

The foundation cards are *never* gathered into the new stock for redealing.

Sometimes tableau cards are gathered for redealing, and in such cases the rules often provide that the new stock be thoroughly shuffled. When only the wastepiles are gathered for redealing, they must not be reshuffled; the order of the cards must not be disturbed.

All exceptions and special conditions are described in full in the text.

"Peeking." By "peeking" we mean looking at the next card from the stock before deciding on the next play. Peeking at a face-down card in a reserve or tableau pile is never permitted by the rules; but, as a general rule, this book sanctions peeking at the next card from the stock. Regardless of what is written in the rules, players will follow their own inclinations as to peeking, but in some cases special reasons support a prohibition of peeking.

Option in play. Unless otherwise stated in the rules, the only obligatory plays are of available cards that start foundation piles. Other plays (including builds on foundations) may be made or not as the player chooses, and alternative plays may be taken in any sequence.

The text in many instances rules that "a space must be filled at once"; in other instances, that "a space may be kept open." We recommend that in all other cases the player adopt a specific rule—either a space must be filled at once, or it may be kept open—according to how difficult he wants to make the particular game.

Solitaires
Played with One Deck

Canfield

(Fascination, Demon, Thirteen)

Time required: 8 minutes   Chance of winning: 1 in 30 games

Layout. Deal a pile of thirteen cards for the reserve. Since only one card at a time should be exposed, the reserve is best dealt face down and then turned face up after the packet is squared up.

Deal the fourteenth card above and to the right of the reserve, for the first foundation. Deal a row of four cards to the right of the reserve, forming the tableau.

Canfield Layout—The $\diamond$ 8 is the first foundation, and other eights, as available, will go in a row to its right; the $\spadesuit$ 9 tops the reserve pile and the tableau is the row at its right. The $\heartsuit$ 10 may be built on $\clubsuit$ J, $\spadesuit$ 9 on $\heartsuit$ 10, and the next card of the reserve moved into the space left by the $\heartsuit$ 10. Customarily, the player holds the stock in his left hand; the wastepile goes below the tableau.

Foundations. As the other three cards of same rank as the first foundation become available, put them in a row with it. Build the foundations up in suit until each pile contains thirteen cards. Ranking of cards is continuous, ace above king and below the two.

Tableau building. On the tableau piles, build downward in alternate colors. The top cards are available for play on foundations, but never into spaces, and an entire pile must be moved as a unit for building on another pile. Fill each space at once with the top card of the reserve. After the reserve is exhausted, fill spaces from the wastepile, but at this time a space may be kept open as long as desired.

Play. The top of the reserve is always available for play on foundations or tableau.

Turn cards up from the stock in batches of three, being careful not to disturb the order within the batch. The top card of each batch is available, and the lower cards as released by play of the upper. Put the cards as turned on a single wastepile.

Redeal. Continue redealing the stock without limit, until the game is blocked or won.

SELECTIVE CANFIELD is the same, except that after the reserve is dealt, five cards are dealt in a row beside it. The player may choose any for his first foundation, the other four becoming the tableau.

Rainbow

Time required: 8 minutes   Chance of winning: 1 in 20 games

Follow all the rules of Canfield except: Turn up cards from the stock one at a time. Two redeals are allowed.

Joker Canfield

Time required: 8 minutes   Chance of winning: 1 in 20 games

This is the same as Canfield, but with the joker added to the deck. Whenever the joker becomes available, it must be played on a foundation as a "wild" card, standing for the next in sequence. Additional cards may be built on the joker. When the natural card becomes available, it is substituted for the joker, which must then be put on top of a foundation pile. If the joker is dealt for the first foundation, call it what you please, naming both rank and suit.

Chameleon

Time required: 8 minutes   Chance of winning: 1 in 30 games

Layout. Deal twelve cards in a pile to form the reserve. Keep this pile squared up so that only the top card is visible. Deal the thirteenth card above the reserve, for the first foundation. Deal three cards in a row to the right of the reserve, forming the tableau.

Chamelon Layout—The ♣ Q is the first foundation, and other queens, as available, will go in a row at its right; the ♡ 7 tops the reserve pile, and the cards at its right are the tableau. The broken lines show the position of the wastepile. The ♡ 7 may be built on the ♣8.

Foundations. Move the other three cards of same rank as the first foundation, as they become available, in a row with it. Build the foundations up in suit until each pile contains thirteen cards. Ranking of cards is continuous, ace above king and below the two.

Tableau building. On the tableau cards build down regardless of suit. Any or all cards may be lifted off a tableau pile for transfer to another. Fill spaces at once from the top of the reserve. After the reserve is exhausted, fill spaces from the wastepile or stock, as desired.

Play. Top cards of the reserve and tableau are always available for building on foundations or tableau. Turn up cards from the stock one at a time, putting unplayable cards in a single wastepile. The top of this pile is always available. There is no redeal.

Pounce

This is Canfield played by two or more players (up to about seven). Each player has his own deck and manipulates his own tableau. (No two decks should be identical in back design.) The foundations are aces, to be moved to the center as they become available. They are common property, played on by all players alike. The winner of a game is he who first gets rid of his reserve pile. As in all multiple solitaire games, strict rules of procedure should be devised and enforced to discourage mayhem, e.g., a player may move cards to the foundations only with one hand.

Elevens

Time required: 2 minutes   Chance of winning: 1 in 4 games

Deal three rows of three cards each. Discard pairs of cards that total eleven. Discard face cards in triplets—one king, one queen, and one jack, of any suits. Fill spaces from the stock. The game is won if you succeed in discarding the entire deck.

Fifteens

Time required: 2 minutes   Chance of winning: 1 in 3 games

Deal sixteen cards, in four rows of four each. Discard kings, queens, jacks, and tens in quartets of the same rank. Discard lower cards in batches that total fifteen—no limitation on the number of cards per batch. Fill spaces from the stock. The game is won if you so discard the entire stock.

Storehouse

(Thirteen Up, The Reserve)

Time required: 5 minutes   Chance of winning: 1 in 3 games

Layout. Remove the four deuces from the deck and put them in a row. Build these foundations up in suit to aces, which rank highest.

Deal thirteen cards in a pile at the left, to form the "storehouse." To the right of it deal a row of cards, forming the tableau.

Storehouse Layout—The ◇ 3 (top of reserve pile) may be built on ◇ 2 in the foundation row; there are no plays in the tableau (row at right of reserve).

Play. On the tableau piles, build downward in suit. Move an entire pile as a unit, for building on another pile. Fill spaces in the tableau at once from the top of the storehouse. After the storehouse is exhausted, fill spaces from wastepile or stock, as desired.

Top cards of the storehouse, tableau, and wastepile are always available for play on foundations or tableau. Turn up cards from the stock one at a time, putting unplayable cards in a single wastepile below the tableau.

Redeals. Two redeals are allowed.

Eagle Wing

(Thirteen Down)

Time required: 4 minutes   Chance of winning: 1 in 20 games

Layout. Deal thirteen cards in a pile, face down, forming the "trunk." Deal eight cards in a row with the trunk, four on each side, forming the "wings." Deal one card in a row above the trunk; this is the first foundation.

Eagle Wing Layout—The ♠ 5 is moved up to the foundation row, beside the ♣ 5, and the top card of the trunk in the center is turned up to fill the space.

Foundations. Move the other cards of same rank as the first foundation, as they become available, into the row with it. Build foundations up in suit until each pile contains thirteen cards. The ace (unless it is the foundation) ranks next above the king.

Play. Cards in the wings are available for play on the foundations. Fill spaces from the trunk, turning the cards face up in the wings. When only one card remains in the trunk, turn it face up; it may be played directly to a foundation without finding space in the wings first. After the trunk is exhausted, fill spaces from wastepile or stock, as you wish.

Turn up cards from the stock one at a time, putting unplayable cards in a single wastepile. The top of this pile is always available.

Redeals. Two redeals are allowed.

Klondike

(Canfield, Fascination, Triangle, Demon Patience, Chinaman)

Time required: 8 minutes   **Chance of winning: 1 in 30 games**

Layout. Deal twenty-eight cards in seven piles, with the number of cards per pile increasing from one to seven from left to right; the top card of each pile being face up, the rest face down. The usual method of dealing is by rows—a face-up card, then six face down at its right; a face-up card on top of the second pile, then five face-down at its right, and so on. These twenty-eight cards form the tableau.

Klondike Layout—The ♣ A is moved to the foundation row (shown by dotted lines). The ♠ 6 may be built on ◇ 7; ◇ K moved into the space left by the ♠ 6; ♠ Q built on ◇ K; and the uncovered face-down cards are turned up.

Foundations. Move all aces, as they become available, to a row above the tableau. Build them up in suit to kings.

Tableau. On the face-up cards in the tableau, build down in alternating colors. The top card of a pile is always available for play on a foundation. All the face-up cards on a pile are moved as a unit when the bottommost of these cards may be built on the top of another pile. (Some players also allow a single card to be moved, even when there are other face-up cards under it.)

Whenever the face-up cards of a pile are cleared off, turn up the next card; it becomes available. A space made by clearing away an entire pile may be filled only by a king (plus the cards, if any, built on the king).

Play. Turn up cards from the stock one at a time, building them on foundations or tableau. Put unplayable cards in a single wastepile. The top of the wastepile is always available. There is no redeal. (Some turn up cards from the stock three at a time, facing them in a fan of which the top card is always available, and go through the stock three times in all. Some go through the stock as in Canfield.)

An ace must be moved into the foundation row as soon as available. But with all other cards you have a choice of building on the foundations or leaving the cards in the tableau to help the manipulation.

Joker Klondike

Time required: 8 minutes   Chance of winning: 1 in 20 games

This is the same as Klondike, but with the joker added to the deck. Whenever the joker becomes available it must be played on a foundation as a "wild" card, standing for the next in sequence. Additional cards may be built on the joker. When the natural card becomes available, it is substituted for the joker, which must then be put on top of a foundation pile. If no foundation has been started at the time the joker first becomes available, it cannot be moved from its position until an ace appears.

Multiple Klondike

This is for two or more players, each playing a game of Klondike simultaneously with the others, and all playing to common foundations. No two decks should be identical in design and color. A player may be required to play an ace. If two or more try to play identical cards to the same foundation pile, the one who gets it down on the pile has made the play and the other must restore his card to where it came from before he may resume play.

Klondike for Two
(Double Solitaire)

Two play, each with his own deck of cards (the two decks must be of different designs or colors). Each manipulates his own tableau, but all foundations form a common pool to which either may play. When the layouts are dealt, the lowest-ranking one-card pile determines the first player; if these cards are of the same rank, the lower of the cards on the two-card piles, and so on. A player's turn ends when he puts a card face up on his wastepile, and his opponent's turn begins. If a player makes any other play when able to play an ace to a foundation, his turn ends there if his opponent stops him before he has completed a subsequent play. The winner is the player who has played the most cards to the foundations, if and when the game becomes blocked.

Agnes

Time required: 5 minutes   Chance of winning: 1 in 3 games

Follow all the rules of Klondike except for these modifications:

Deal the twenty-ninth card above the tableau to make the first foundation. Build foundations up in suit, ace ranking between king and two, until each pile contains thirteen cards. Below the tableau deal a row of seven cards, forming the reserve. These cards are available for play on foundations and tableau. Whenever play comes to a standstill deal another row of seven cards on the reserve, forming piles. Do not fill spaces in the reserve except by subsequent deals. Only the top card of a reserve pile is available. Turn the last two cards of the deck face up; both are available.

A space in the tableau may be filled only by a card of rank next-lower to the foundations.

Whitehead

Time required: 8 minutes   Chance of winning: 1 in 20 games

Follow all the rules of Klondike except for these modifications:

Deal the entire tableau face up, overlapping the cards downward in column so that all may be inspected. On the tableau, build down in color (red on red, black on black, regardless of suits). A space may be filled by any available card or build. All cards on top of a tableau pile that are in sequence in the same *suit* may be lifted off as a unit, for transfer to another pile.

Thumb and Pouch

Time required: 5 minutes Chance of winning: 1 in 4 games

Follow all the rules of Klondike except for these modifications as to building in the tableau:

Either the top card of a pile, or all the face-up cards as a unit, may be moved. A card may be built on a card of next-higher rank, of any suit but its own. A space may be filled by any available card or build.

Spiderette

Time required: 8 minutes Chance of winning: 1 in 20 games

Layout. Deal twenty-eight cards in a tableau as for Klondike.

Play. There are no foundations; all building is on the tableau. Build down in sequence, ending at ace, regardless of suits (but prefer to build in suit when choice offers). The top card of each pile is available. Cards at the top of a pile that are in correct sequence in the same suit may be lifted as a unit to be built elsewhere. When a face-down card is bared, turn it face up; it becomes available. A space made by removing an entire pile may be filled by any available card or build.

Whenever play comes to a standstill, deal another row of seven cards on the seven piles. Any spaces must be filled prior to the deal. Put the last three cards of the deck on the first three piles.

The object of the play is to get all thirteen cards of a suit in correct sequence on top of a pile. Whenever you so assemble a suit, discard it from the tableau. The game is won if you assemble all four suits.

Will o' the Wisp

Time required: 8 minutes Chance of winning: 1 in 4 games

This is the same is Spiderette, except that the layout comprises only twenty-one cards, in seven piles of three cards each, with only the top card of each pile face up.

Westcliff

Time required: 5 minutes   Chance of winning: 9 out of 10 games

Layout. Deal thirty cards in a tableau, a row of ten piles of three cards each, with only the top card of each pile face up. The usual way of dealing is by rows, two face down and the last face up.

Westcliff Layout—The ♣A has been moved to the foundation row and other aces will go beside it. The ♣2 may be built on ♣A, ♠2 on ♦3, ♦6 on ♠7, ♦7 on ♠8, and cards below them turned up.

Foundations. Move the aces, as they become available, to a row above the tableau. Build them up in suit to kings.

Tableau building. On the tableau, build down in alternating colors. The top of a pile, or all face-up cards in correct sequence and alternation when the bottommost of such cards is suitable, may be lifted as a unit for building on the top of another pile, or to fill a space made by removal of an entire pile. Top cards of the piles are always available for play on foundations. When a face-down card on the tableau is bared, turn it face up; it becomes available.

Play. Turn up cards from the stock one at a time, playing them on foundations or tableau. Put unplayed cards in a single wastepile. The top of this pile is always available. There is no redeal.

Easthaven
(Aces Up)

Time required: 5 minutes   Chance of winning: 1 in 4 games

Follow all the rules of Westcliff except for these modifications:

Deal only seven piles for the tableau, twenty-one cards in all. A space may be filled only by a king, or a build with a king at the bottom. Whenever play comes to a standstill, deal another row of seven cards on the tableau. All spaces in the tableau must be filled (if possible) before a new row is dealt. Put the last three cards of the deck in a row on the first three tableau piles.

Pyramid
(Pile of Twenty-eight)

Time required: 4 minutes   Chance of winning: 1 in 50 games

Layout. Deal twenty-eight cards in the form of a pyramid. (See diagram.) This comprises seven rows, the successive rows increasing from one to seven and overlapping so that each card (except in the seventh row) is partly covered by two cards of the next row. At the outset, the seven cards of the last row are available. The removal of any two adjacent cards uncovers one card in the row above. Each card wholly uncovered becomes available.

Play. From the available cards, discard pairs of cards that total thirteen. Discard kings singly. (In the diagram, the following may be discarded: diamond king; spade three and diamond ten; club eight and heart five. Then, with the help of newly-released cards: club queen and spade ace; diamond seven and heart six.)

Turn cards from the stock one at a time, putting unplayable cards in a wastepile. The top of this pile is always available. It may be paired with the next card turned from the stock, or with any released card in the pyramid.

The game is won if you get all the cards into the discard pile.

PAR PYRAMID is a method of scoring Pyramid that establishes degrees of victory. Two redeals are allowed. If you win the game in one deal, score 50. If you clear away the pyramid on the first deal, use the redeals to deplete the stock, if possible, and score 50 less the number of cards left in the wastepile. Similarly, if you clear away the pyramid on the second or third deal, score 35 or 20 respectively, less the number in the wastepile. If you do not clear away the pyramid, subtract from your score the total number of cards left undiscarded.

"Par" is a net score of zero in six games, and any net plus may be considered a win. Par Pyramid may be played competitively by two or more, each playing six games with his own deck. The best final net score wins.

Thirteens

(Simple Addition)

Time required: 2 minutes   Chance of winning: 1 in 2 games

Deal two rows of five cards each. Pick out pairs of cards that total thirteen and put them in a discard pile; as, 8 and 5; jack and 2; queen and ace. Discard kings singly. Fill spaces from the stock. The game is won if you succeed in dealing the entire deck.

Beleaguered Castle

(Sham Battle, Laying Siege)

Time required: 15 minutes   Chance of winning: 1 in 3 games

Foundations. Remove the four aces from the deck and put them in a column. Build these foundations up in suit to kings.

Beleaguered Castle Layout—The blank outlines represent cards dealt face up.

Tableau. Deal the remainder of the deck in two wings of the tableau, one on each side of the aces. Each wing comprises four rows of six cards each. Overlap the cards in each row, so that all are visible but only one at a time is available. The usual method of dealing is by columns, alternately to the left and right wings.

Play. On the tableau, build downward regardless of suit. One card at a time may be lifted from a row and built on a foundation or on the uppermost card of any other row. Only the uppermost card of each row is available. A space made by removing an entire row may be filled by any available card.

Tips. Make no move until you have planned a complete line of play that will create a space. If you cannot find a way to do that, the game is probably hopeless. Do not build on foundations merely because you can. Building some foundations ahead of others may cause a block: the higher cards played here may be indispensable for tableau building, to release the lower cards wanted on other foundations. The ideal is to keep all four foundations abreast. It is always safe to play a two or three to a foundation, but thereafter build on foundations only when you can keep them abreast, or when compelled to do so in order to release buried cards.

Streets and Alleys

Time required: 15 minutes   Chance of winning: 1 in 4 games

This follows the rules of Beleaguered Castle, except that the entire deck is dealt into the tableau. The upper four rows comprise seven cards each, the lower four, six each. Space is left between the rows for the foundations. The aces are moved into the foundations column as they become available.

Citadel

Time required: 15 minutes   Chance of winning: 1 in 3 games

This is the same as Beleaguered Castle after the deal, but differs in the layout as follows: Do not remove aces from the deck, but commence dealing to the tableau (in columns).

Whenever you turn an ace, place it in the foundations column instead of on the tableau. Build as you can on the foundations, in the course of dealing, with the proviso that only a newly-turned card may be put on a foundation, not a card already on the tableau. Whenever you put a card on a foundation, skip the row where it would have gone on the tableau. The completed rows thus will not be uniform in length.

Fortress

Time required: 15 minutes   Chance of winning: 1 in 10 games

Layout. Deal the entire deck in two wings of a tableau. Each wing comprises five rows, an upper row of six cards and four rows of five. Overlap the cards in each row so that only one card at a time is available. The usual method of dealing is by columns.

Play. Move the four aces, as they become available, to a column between the wings. Build these foundations up in suit to kings. On the tableau, build in suit, either up or down as you please. (You may build up on one row and down on another.) One card at a time—the uppermost card of a row—may be lifted from the tableau to be built on foundations or other tableau rows.

Chessboard
(Fives)

Time required: 15 minutes   Chance of winning: 1 in 5 games

Follow all the rules of Fortress, except that you have your choice of foundations. After dealing the tableau, look it over and decide on the rank of your foundations according to what will best promote manipulation of the tableau.

Decade

Time required: 2 minutes   Chance of winning: 1 in 50 games

Deal the entire deck in a row, one card at a time. As you go along, toss into the discard any two or more adjacent cards that total ten, twenty, or thirty. Count the kings, queens, and jacks as ten each. To win the game you must discard all the cards but one.

Fortress Layout—The blank outlines represent cards dealt face up. The aces, as they become available, will be moved into the spaces indicated by the broken outlines.

Suspense

Time required: 10 minutes　　　Chance of winning: 1 in 6 games

Layout. Deal twenty-four cards in four groups of six cards each. Form each group as shown in the diagram. The face-down card is the "center"; the two cards on either side of the center, in each group, are the "wings."

Suspense—The layout consists of four such groups.

Wastepile. Turn up cards from the stock one at a time and put them in a single wastepile. At the beginning of play, the only possible builds are from the layout to the wastepile. On the top card of the wastepile build in sequence up or down regardless of suits. You may change direction as often as you please, it always being permissible to place a card on the next-higher or -lower ranking card. Sequence of rank is continuous, ace being below the two and above the king.

At first, only four cards in the layout are available, the uppermost card of each group. Lower cards become available as the upper are played off to the wastepile.

Foundations. The four center cards are foundations. As each is unburied, move it to a column at the left. Build up in suit on each foundation. Of course, not all four suits will necessarily be represented; in such case, combine foundation piles of the same suit when they are built to the meeting point. Available for foundation-building are: any card of the layout not covered, the top of the wastepile, and a card turned from the stock. It is not compulsory to build when able, but cards on the foundations may not be moved elsewhere.

Tableau. Wing cards belong to the tableau. As each is unburied, move it to the right side of the layout. On tableau cards, build down in suit, and combine piles of the same suit when they are built to the meeting point.

A tableau pile may be reversed upon a foundation of the same suit, when the two piles have been built to the meeting point. When the foundations lack one or more suits, these suits must be built up entirely in the tableau.

In the event (very unlikely) that one or more suits are entirely missing from the foundations and wing cards, all cards of those suits may be discarded from the deck as soon as the fact is discovered. (Discard them in dealing, as they turn up in the stock.)

A wing card may be built on the wastepile, provided that another card of the same suit is visible at that time among the foundation or tableau cards. Such sacrifice of a wing card is in general poor policy, but might be necessary to uncover quickly some cards still buried in the layout.

Redeals. Two redeals are allowed.

You win the game when all cards are built on foundations or tableau.

Tips. Don't worry about the direction of builds in the wastepile. Uncover wing and foundation cards as fast as possible, without sacrificing wing cards. Normally, the layout should be completely dissolved well before the end of the first deal. Don't overlook opportunities to play from the layout to such foundations and tableau cards as you have uncovered; such moves are of course preferable to loading the wastepile.

Flower Garden

(The Garden, Bouquet)

Time required: 15 minutes   Chance of winning: 1 in 2 games

Layout. Deal a "garden" (tableau) of thirty-six cards, in six rows of six. Overlap the rows, forming six piles spread downward. Spread the remaining sixteen cards below the garden to form the "bouquet" (reserve).

Flower Garden Layout—The piles of cards above are the tableau; the fan of cards below is the reserve. All cards are dealt face up.

Foundations. Move the four aces, as they become available, to a row above the garden. Build them up in suit to kings.

Play. On the columns of the garden, build down regardless of suits. One card at a time may be lifted from the top of a pile and played on a foundation or on the top card of another pile. A space made by removing a whole column of the garden may be filled by any available card. Every card of the bouquet is available at all times for play on foundations or garden.

Tips. Do not use bouquet cards for building in the garden if avoidable, for to do so permanently decreases the number of cards available at one time. For the same reason, a space is not an unmixed blessing. Loading up the other columns to make a space may prove too costly. Aim primarily to release all the aces, twos, and threes, for the immolation of a single low card may block the game.

King Albert

(Idiot's Delight)

Time required: 15 minutes   Chance of winning: 1 in 2 games

Layout. Deal forty-five cards in a tableau of nine piles of overlapping cards, spread downward, the number of cards per pile increasing from one to nine. It is easiest to deal by rows.

Below this tableau spread the remaining seven cards of the deck, forming the reserve.

King Albert Layout—All cards are dealt face up.

Foundations. Move the four aces, as they become available, to a row above the tableau. Build them up in suit to kings.

Play. On the tableau piles, build down in alternate colors. One card at a time may be lifted from the top of a pile to be built on foundations or on the top card of another pile. A space made by removing an entire pile may be filled by any available card. All cards of the reserve are available for play on foundations or tableau.

Yukon

Time required: 8 minutes   Chance of winning: 1 in 4 games

Layout. Deal twenty-eight cards in seven piles, as for Klondike. Deal the remaining twenty-four cards evenly upon the six piles other than the single card. Overlap all the face-up cards downward, so that all may be seen.

Foundations. Move the four aces, as they become available, to a row above the tableau. Build them up in suit to kings.

Play. On the top card of a tableau pile may be built a next-lower card of opposite color, except that no build may be made on an ace. An ace at the top of a pile must be moved at once to the foundation row, but it is not compulsory to build higher cards on the foundations; such cards may be kept in the tableau for building.

Any card in the tableau, no matter how deeply buried, may be moved to make a build; all the cards covering it are moved with it as a unit.

On clearing a face-down card, turn it face up; it then becomes available. Top cards of all piles are available for building on foundations.

A space made by clearing away an entire pile may be filled only by a king. For this purpose any king in sight is available, all covering cards being moved with it as a unit.

Tips. Aim first of all to uncover the face-down cards. Build on foundations only as an aid to manipulating the tableau. Be wary of building any foundation far ahead of another, lest cards vital for building be put out of reach.

La Belle Lucie

(The Fan, Clover Leaf, Midnight Oil, Alexander the Great)

Time required: 15 minutes   Chance of winning: 1 in 10 games

Layout. Deal the whole deck in seventeen fans (piles spread so that all cards are visible) of three cards each. The card left over forms a separate pile.

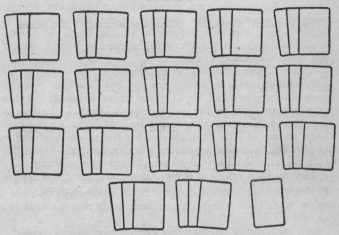

La Belle Lucie Layout—All cards are dealt face up.

Foundations. Move the four aces, as they become available, to a row near you. Build these foundations up in suit to kings.

Play. On the tableau fans, build down in suit. One card at a time may be lifted from a fan to be put on a foundation or another fan. Spaces made by playing off a whole fan are not filled.

Redeals. Two redeals are allowed. After play has come to a standstill, gather all the cards not on the foundations, shuffle them, and deal again in fans of three. If one or two cards are left over, they make a separate fan.

Draw. After the last redeal, any one buried card may be drawn out of any one fan.

Tips. Once a build is made, it cannot be unmade except by play on a foundation. Therefore make no build until you have assured yourself that (a) the cards below, thereby immolated, are not needed, or cannot be released anyhow; or (b) the build is sure to find eventual place on a foundation; or (c) burying the cards beyond recovery, to release others, is a worthwhile investment.

One way to begin, after the deal, is to note all the cards buried by kings. Since the cards next-lower in sequence to these buried cards cannot be moved, they can be built upon without further ado. For example, if the ten of spades is below a king, build on the nine of spades. Similarly, having immolated some cards by a build, proceed to build freely on the cards next-lower in suit.

The layout usually offers many choices of play. Canvass all possibilities before making a move. For example, suppose that the four, five and six of clubs are available. If the five and four are built on the six, that fan is killed. If the four is first built on the five, that pile is killed, while the six can perhaps be moved later through clearing the seven. The choice of play will of course depend on whether the cards below the club five or below the club six are wanted more urgently.

Play on foundations at every opportunity, since if a card is playable on a foundation it is of no use in the tableau.

Trefoil

This is the same as La Belle Lucie, except that the four aces are removed from the deck in advance and put in the foundation row. The first tableau comprises sixteen fans of three.

Shamrocks

(Three-card Fan)

Time required: 15 minutes   Chance of winning: 1 in 4 games

Layout. Deal the whole deck in seventeen fans of three cards each, with one card left over. (See diagram of La Belle Lucie.) If you find any king above another card of the same suit, transfer it below that card.

Foundations. Move the four aces, as they become available, for a foundation row. Build them up in suit to kings.

Play. On the tableau fans, build in sequence, up or down as you wish, regardless of suits. (You may build both ways on the same pile.) But no fan may comprise more than three cards. One card at a time may be lifted off a fan, for play on foundations or another fan. A space made by playing off an entire fan is never filled.

Tips. The layout is a block if you do not find an ace on top of one of the fans and if no available card can be built upon the single card. It is suggested that in such case, to save redealing, you draw out one of the buried aces.

Do not build on foundations merely because you can—you may thereby deprive the tableau of cards vital for building. The ideal way to avoid this self-made block is to keep the four foundations abreast.

Once a fan is gone, you have one less pile for building. Never move the last card of a fan onto another fan, and play it to a foundation only when the move is perfectly safe (the foundations are abreast) or urgently necessary (to break an impasse).

Hit or Miss

(Treize, Roll Call, Talkative, Harvest)

Time required: 15 minutes   Chance of winning: 1 in 50 games

Deal cards one at a time into one pile, calling "Ace" for the first card, "Two" for the second, and so on. After "King," call the next card "Ace," and so through the deck.

When a card proves to be of the rank you call, it is *hit*. Discard all hit cards from the deck. The object of play is to hit every card in the deck—eventually.

Whenever the stock is exhausted, turn over the wastepile to form a new stock, and continue counting from where you left off. The game is construed lost if you go through the stock twice in succession without a hit. (The point of this rule is that unlimited redealing would surely win the game unless a no-hit were encountered when the stock comprises 52, 39, 26 or 13 cards.)

Stalactites

(Old Mole, Grampus)

Time required: 8 minutes   Chance of winning: 5 out of 6 games

Layout. Deal a row of four cards for foundations. Turn these cards sidewise, so that when cards are built on them in the normal way the base cards will always be identifiable.

Below the foundations, deal the rest of the deck in a tableau of six rows of eight cards each, the cards overlapping to form eight piles spread downward.

Stalactites Layout—All cards are dealt face up, the foundations in the row of horizontal cards above, the tableau piles below. Cards played on the foundations will be placed in normal (vertical) position.

Foundations. Inspect the layout and decide whether to build the foundations by ones or twos, e.g., 7, 8, 9, 10, J, or 7, 9, J, K, 2, 4, etc. The decision applies to all four foundations. Build them up by the chosen interval, ignoring suits, until each pile contains thirteen cards. (The visible base card warns you when to stop.)

Play. Only the top card of each pile is available, but two cards may be removed from anywhere in the tableau and held out in a reserve, with the proviso that the reserve may never comprise more than two cards. The reserve cards are also available for building on foundations. Spaces made by removal of an entire tableau column are never filled.

Auld Lang Syne
(Patience)

Time required: 2 minutes   Chance of winning: 1 in 100 games

Layout. Remove the four aces from the deck and put them in a row. These are foundations, to be built up to kings regardless of suits.

Auld Lang Syne Layout—There is no available play from the reserve (lower row) to the foundations, so another reserve row must be dealt on the first.

Play. Deal the stock into four reserve piles, one row of four cards at a time. Afer dealing each batch of four, play up what you can from the tops of the reserve piles onto the foundations. Cards in the reserve piles become available when they are uncovered, but may not be used to fill spaces. There is no redeal.

Old Patience
(Try Again, Sir Tommy)

Time required: 5 minutes   Chance of winning: 1 in 5 games

Foundations. Move the four aces, as they become available, into a row. Build each ace up to king, regardless of suits.

Play. Turn up cards from the stock one at a time, placing each on any of four wastepiles. After each batch of four cards, pause and play up what you can from the wastepiles to the foundations. Only the top card of each pile is available.

Tips. When placing a card on a wastepile, prefer to place it on a higher card than on a lower card. When this policy is not feasible, place a card on a pile that does not contain another card of the same rank. But this rule has its exceptions: Most vital of all is to avoid burying all four cards of one rank under higher cards.

Puss In Corner—The ♣ 2 may be built on either the ♣ A or the ♠ A.

Puss in Corner

Time required: 10 minutes   Chance of winning: 1 in 3 games

Foundations. Remove the four aces from the deck and put them in a square. These are foundations, to be built up in color to kings. (Red on red, black on black, otherwise regardless of suits.)

Play. Turn up cards from the stock one at a time, placing them on any of four wastepiles. (These piles are traditionally placed at the four corners of the foundation-square, thus giving the game its name.) After each batch of four cards, pause and play up what you can from the piles to the foundations. Only the top card of each pile is available.

Redeal. One redeal is allowed. Pick up the wastepiles in any prefixed order, as clockwise from the lower left corner.

Tips. See OLD PATIENCE.

Accordion

(Idle Year, Tower of Babel, Methuselah)

Time required: 5 minutes   Chance of winning: 1 in 100 games

Deal the entire deck in a row, one card at a time. A card may be moved upon its left-hand neighbor, or upon the card third to its left, if the two cards concerned, are of same suit or rank. A pile of two or more cards is moved as a unit, the legality of the move depending on its top card. The game is won if the entire deck is gotten into one pile.

Accordion—$\diamond$ 5 may be moved onto $\diamond$ 4, then both on $\spadesuit$ 5, then $\heartsuit$ Q on $\heartsuit$ 10.

Tips. With choice of plays, before making any play deal a few more cards to see if there is a choice.

Four Seasons

(Corner Card, Vanishing Cross)

Time required: 5 minutes   Chance of winning: 1 in 10 games

Layout. Deal a tableau of five cards in the form of a cross. Deal the sixth card in one corner of the cross, forming the first foundation.

Four Seasons Layout—The ♣ J is the first foundation; the other cards are the tableau. The ◇ 5 may be built on the ♡ 6.

Foundations. Put the other three cards of same rank as the first foundation, when they become available, in the remaining corners of the cross. Build the foundations up in suit (ace ranking next above king) until each pile contains thirteen cards.

Tableau building. Build down regardless of suit; a king may be played on an ace, unless aces are foundations. One card at a time may be moved from the top of a pile elsewhere. Fill spaces with any available cards from tableau, wastepile, or stock.

Play. Turn cards up from stock one at a time, playing them on foundations or tableau. Put unplayable cards in a single wastepile. The top of this pile is always available.

Simplicity

Time required: 5 minutes   Chance of winning: 9 out of 10 games

This is the same as Four Seasons except: The tableau is two rows of six cards each. Deal the thirteenth card for the first foundation. On the tableau, build down in alternating colors.

Baker's Dozen

Time required: 15 minutes   Chance of winning: 2 out of 3 games

Layout. Deal the entire deck in four rows of thirteen cards each, overlapping the rows to form piles of cards spread downward. Then transfer every king to the bottom of its pile.

Baker's Dozen Layout—The ♠ K will be put under the ◇ 3. All the outlines represent other face-up cards.

Foundations. Move the four aces, as they become available, to a row above the tableau. Build them up in suit to kings.

Play. One card at a time may be lifted from the top of a pile and built on a foundation or on the top card of another pile.

On the tableau, build down regardless of suit. A space made by removing a whole pile may not be filled.

Tips. Take note of every card that lies over (in sense of availability) a lower card of the same unit. Whether or no any cards intervene between the two, this situation is a reversal that must be resolved by tableau building. Aim primarily to straighten out every one of these "kinks." Be wary of building one foundation ahead of another: a block may result for lack of a builder moved prematurely to a foundation.

Good Measure

Time required: 15 minutes   Chance of winning: 2 out of 3 games

This follows all the rules of Baker's Dozen, except that the first two aces turned up in dealing are put at once in the foundation row instead of the tableau, and the latter is dealt in five rows, making ten spread piles of five cards each.

Little Spider

Time required: 20 minutes   Chance of winning: 2 out of 3 games

Layout. Deal the whole deck into eight piles, dealt as two rows of four with room between for a row of foundations. All cards are dealt face up. After dealing each batch of eight cards, one to each pile, pause and play what you can on the foundations. The last four cards of the deck go on the top row.

Foundations. Move the two aces of one color, and the two kings of the other color, as they turn up during the deal, into the foundation row. You can choose red aces and black kings, or black aces and red kings, as you wish. Build the aces up in suit to kings, and the kings down in suit to aces.

Play. During the deal, a foundation ace or king may be moved into place from either the upper or lower row of the tableau. From the upper row, playable cards may be transferred to any foundations. From a tableau pile of the lower row, however, an additional card may be played up only to the foundation directly above it.

Little Spider Layout—The cards in the top and bottom rows are the tops of tableau piles; the cards in the middle row are the foundations.

After the deal is complete, the top card of every pile is available for play on all foundations and all other piles. On the tableau, build in sequence up or down as you please, regardless of suits. The sequence here is continuous, the ace ranking below the two and above the king. A space made by removing an entire pile may not be filled.

Tips. Don't hurry to build up the foundations; save cards as long as possible for tableau building. Try to bring together cards of the same suit, built in sequence opposite from the direction of the foundation of that suit, so that in due time they can all be skimmed off.

Royal Flush

Time required: 2 minutes   Chance of winning: 1 in 5 games

As in poker, the royal flush is ace, king, queen, jack and ten of the same suit.

Deal the entire deck into a row of five piles, face down, putting the two extra cards on the first two piles.

Turn over the first pile and discard its cards one by one (if necessary) until any card of rank ten or higher appears. This card fixes the suit of the royal flush. For example, if the first card of sufficient rank is $\heartsuit$ 10, the royal flush will be $\heartsuit$ A K Q J 10. If no high card shows in the first pile, go on to the second pile, etc., until one shows.

With the suit fixed, turn over the next pile and discard its cards until you reach a card of the royal flush; then do the same with each remaining pile. When a pile contains no flush card, it is discarded entire. (It may be easier to fan out the piles, face up, and discard all cards that lie above any card of the flush.)

Turn the piles face down and gather them into a new stock, reversing the order in which they were dealt before—putting each pile on the one at its left. Deal the new stock into four piles, as far as the cards will go. Turn them over (or fan them) again, and discard all cards on top of the royal flush cards, as before. Reversing the order again, gather them into a new stock, face down, and deal three piles; again turn the piles face up and discard down to the royal flush cards. Gather them, reversing the order again, deal two piles, and discard as before.

The game is won if now only the five cards of the royal flush remain, and no other.

Royal Marriage

(Betrothal, Matrimony, Coquette)

Time required: 4 minutes   Chance of winning: 1 in 2 games

Put the king of hearts on the bottom of the deck, and the queen of hearts on the table at your left. Deal the entire deck in a row with the queen, one card at a time. As you go along, discard any one card or any two adjacent cards that are enclosed by two cards of the same suit or rank. The game is won if you get the royal couple, king and queen of hearts, side by side.

Clock

(Hidden Cards, Four of a Kind, Travelers, Sun Dial)

Time required: 3 minutes   Chance of winning: 1 in 100 games

Layout. Deal the deck into thirteen piles of four cards each, face down. Traditionally, the piles should be arranged like a clock dial—twelve packets in a circle, the thirteenth in the center. In any event, the piles must be construed to be numbered from one to thirteen.

Play. Turn up the top card of the thirteen pile (center of the clock face). Put it face up under the pile of its own number, jack counting as 11, queen as 12, king as 13, ace as 1. For example, if it is the six of clubs, put it under the sixth pile, the pile at "six o'clock." Turn up the top of the six pile and put it under the pile of its own number. Continue in this way, putting a card under a pile and then turning up the top card of that pile. If the last face-down card of any pile belongs to that pile, turn next the face-down card of the next pile clockwise around the circle.

The game is won if all thirteen piles become transmuted into fours-of-a-kind. It is lost if the fourth king is turned up before all other fours are completed.

Watch

Time required: 3 minutes   Chance of winning: 1 in 20 games

Follow all the rules of Clock, but if you are blocked before the game is won, draw any one face-down card, exchange it for the king just turned, and continue play. If the king again turns up before all other fours are completed, the game is lost.

Grandfather's Clock

Time required: 8 minutes   Chance of winning: 3 out of 4 games

Foundations. Take from the deck the following twelve cards: two of hearts, three of spades, four of diamonds, five of clubs, six of hearts, seven of spades, eight of diamonds, nine of clubs, ten of hearts, jack of spades, queen of diamonds, king of clubs. Put them in a circle corresponding to the hours on a clock dial, with the nine of clubs at "twelve o'clock" and the rest in sequence around the circle.

Build each foundation up in suit until it reaches the number appropriate to its position on the clock. Jack represents 11, queen 12, king 13, and ace 1. The sequence of rank is continuous, with ace below two and above king. The ten, jack, queen, and king foundations will each require the addition of four cards; all others will take three cards.

Grandfather's Clock Layout—All cards are dealt face up.

Tableau. Deal the rest of the deck into five rows of eight cards each. Overlap the rows to form piles of cards spread downward.

Play. The top card of each tableau pile is available for play on a foundation or on the top card of another pile. On the tableau, build down regardless of suit. A space made by playing off a whole pile may be filled by any available card.

Rondo

(Eight-Day Clock, Perpetual Motion)

Time required: 20 minutes   Chance of winning: 1 in 20 games

Layout. Deal the deck into thirteen piles of four cards each, face up. The piles must be construed as numbered from one to thirteen. Arrange them in whatever array you find most helpful in keeping track of the numbers.

Rondo Layout—The ♣ A may not be moved, since it tops the pile of its own number; the ♡ 4 may not be moved to the 3 pile, so it is put under the 4 pile and the ◇ Q put under the 5 pile, etc.

Play. The whole play consists in "weaving." Move the top card of pile 1 below pile 2; the top card of pile 2 below pile 3; and so on around the circuit. From pile 13 return to pile 1. But when a pile is topped by a card of its own number (counting jack 11, queen 12, king 13, ace 1) you neither move its top card nor put a card under it; you skip that pile and go to the next available pile beyond.

The effect of the transfer is (usually) to bring more and more cards to the tops of like-numbered piles, so decreasing the circuit of piles included in the transfers. When finally each of the thirteen piles is topped by a card of its own number, lift off and discard these thirteen top cards.

The last card removed before this happy event has for the moment "nowhere to go." Lay it aside until the thirteen top cards are discarded. Then resume play by putting it under the pile of its own number (or the first thereafter which is available under the rule).

Continue play in the same way; the game is won if you discard three sets of thirteen cards.

Perpetual Motion

(Idiot's Delight)

Time required: 60 minutes   Chance of winning: 1 in 4 games

Deal a row of four cards. If two or three are of the same rank, move the others upon the leftmost of the equal cards. Deal another row of four upon the first. Move cards if you can, so as to bring equal cards together leftward. Continue dealing the pack in batches of four, making what plays you can after each deal. If all four cards dealt in a row are of the same rank, discard them and deal another row.

After you have run through the deck, put the rightmost pile on its left neighbor; put this augmented pile on the one at the left, and then the triple pile on the leftmost. Turn the cards face down to form a new stock, and continue play as before. Be careful not to shuffle, or let the cards become disarranged, once the game has begun. Redeal without limit, until the game is decided.

Each time you deal a row of four cards that prove to be all of the same rank, discard these four cards from the deck. The game is won if you eventually discard the entire deck in batches of four.

When the deck is reduced to twelve or eight cards, fan it out before the first deal and observe the order of the cards. If this identical order recurs at some later time, resign the game.

Osmosis after several plays. Any club, when it becomes available, may be played to the top foundation row (on the ♣ 8); only the ◇ 4 could be played, at this point, to the second foundation row; the ten of spades or the ten of hearts could be played to the third foundation row (indicated by broken lines below the ◇ 10–8).

Osmosis

(Treasure Trove)

Time required: 5 minutes   Chance of winning: 1 in 8 games

Layout. Deal four piles of four cards each, in a column at the left. Since only the top card of each pile should be known, the cards are best dealt face down and then turned face up after the packets are squared up.

Foundations. Deal one card at the right of the top reserve pile. This is the first foundation. Put the other cards of same rank, as they become available, in a column below the first.

Build each foundation in suit, regardless of order. Put the cards in a row with the foundation, overlapping, so that all are visible. On the first foundation, any card of the same suit may be built as soon as it becomes available. On each lower foundation, a card may be built only if a card of the same rank has been built on the foundation above. For example, suppose that the first foundation is the jack of diamonds, and the second is the jack of spades. Finding the seven, four, and king of diamonds available, you have piled them on the jack. You may continue putting any diamonds on the foundation, but at the moment the only spades you may put on the spade jack are the four, seven, and king.

Play. Top cards of the reserve piles are available for play on foundations. Turn up cards from the stock in batches of three. Do not disturb the order of the cards in counting off these batches. The top card of the batch is available, also the lower cards if released by play of the upper. Put each residue of unplayable cards in a single wastepile. Redeal without limit until the game is blocked, or is won by getting the entire deck onto the foundations.

Peek

Follow the rules of Osmosis, but spread the reserve piles so that all cards may be seen. Sight of the entire reserve often curtails play by revealing a hopeless block. Sometimes it enables a block to be avoided by withholding one foundation card until another becomes available.

Scorpion

Time required: 8 minutes   Chance of winning: 1 in 10 games

Layout. Deal seven cards in a row, four face down and three
face up. Deal two more rows in the same way; then four more

Scorpion Layout—The $\diamondsuit$ 8, $\diamondsuit$ Q, $\clubsuit$ 2 and $\clubsuit$ 9 may be moved as
a unit to the $\diamondsuit$ 9, and the card below the $\diamondsuit$ 8 turned up; the $\diamondsuit$ 3
may be moved to the $\diamondsuit$ 4; etc.

rows with all the cards face up. Overlap the rows to form
piles of cards spread downward.

The forty-nine cards so dealt make the tableau. Leave the
three remaining cards face down, as a reserve.

Play. All building is confined to the tableau, there being no
separate foundations. The object of play is to reduce the
tableau to four piles, one of each suit, with the cards of each
suit in sequence, the king at the bottom of the pile.

On the top card of each pile may be placed the next-lower
card of the same suit; nothing may be built on an ace. Any
card in the tableau, no matter how deeply buried, may be
moved to make a build; but all the cards above it must be
moved with it as a unit.

On clearing a face-down card, turn it face up; it then becomes available.

A space made by clearing away an entire pile may be filled only by a king. Any king in sight is available for this purpose, all covering cards being moved with it as a unit.

Reserve. After play comes to a standstill, deal the three reserve cards, one on the top of each of the three leftmost piles. Resume play; if the game again becomes blocked, it is lost.

Tips. Look at each face-up card that covers a face-down card. Trace backwards to see if it can be removed. For example, suppose one of such cards to be the eight of diamonds. Look for the nine of diamonds. If you find it, note the card that covers it, say the queen of clubs. Look for the king of clubs—and so on. The first objective is to make a series of moves that will uncover face-down cards. Often there is choice which way to "break" two piles—as, the second pile on the fourth, or the fourth on the second. Some builds will preclude others. All such choices should be made primarily to get at the buried cards.

Similarly, when you have a space, trace the series of plays that would follow; the proper choice of king may create another space.

You do not have to fill the spaces before dealing the reserve cards. With no positive advantage in sight from using a space —such as uncovering a buried card or making another space— hold the first space until you see the reserve cards. For this purpose, maneuver to keep a space among the four piles at the right, not among the three at the left.

The game will inevitably become blocked if the tableau contains a "reversed sequence" or a "criss-cross"—for example, spade queen, spade jack, spade king, adjacent in that order down a pile; or club ten directly on heart four and heart three directly on club jack. Careless play may create an impasse where none existed before. Suppose that the end cards of two piles (reading down) are four of diamonds, six of diamonds (on one pile); five of diamonds, three of diamonds (on the other). To build the three on the four will make a block. The right way is to build the four on the five, then the five on the six, then the three on the four.

Moojub

Time required: 4 minutes   Chance of winning: 1 in 2 games

Layout. Deal a column of four cards at the left, forming a reserve.

Foundations. The number of foundation cards depends upon chance—the more such cards, the better the chance of winning the game. The foundations must be put in columns to the right of the reserve.

At the top of the first foundation column, put the lowest-ranking card that shows in the reserve. Below it must go the lowest-ranking available card of a *different* suit; below that a third suit, and below that the fourth, forming the first foundation column of four cards of different suits, each card being the lowest of its suit available at that time. (Ace is ranked low, under the two.)

The first foundation column fixes the suits; thereafter, each foundation column must be formed of the four suits in the same order.

On every foundation card, build up in suit with the ranking of cards continuous, ace above king and below the two.

Play. Continue dealing the stock in batches of four, one card on each reserve pile. The top card of each pile is available. Whenever an available card can be built on a foundation pile, it must be so built. When no build is possible, available cards may be placed in position as new foundation cards, always provided that—

(1) Each foundation column must comprise cards of all four suits before a new column may be started; and foundation cards must be put out in order from top to bottom;

(2) Each new foundation card must be of the same suit as the card at its left;

(3) With choice of available cards to make a new foundation, the lowest of the suit must be taken.

A space in the reserve is never filled except by the subsequent deal of four cards.

The game is won if, after the stock is exhausted, all the cards have been gotten into the foundation rows.

Moojub after several plays. The column at the extreme left is the reserve; all other cards are foundations. The ♣ 6 may be played beside the ♣ 3; then the ♣ 7 on the ♣ 6; then the ♠ A beside the ♠ 5. If these plays have uncovered a heart, the lowest such heart (other than the ♡ 3 or ♡ A) may be played as a new foundation beside the ♡ K.

Block Eleven

(Calling Out)

Time required: 1 minute   Chance of winning: 1 in 5 games

Deal twelve cards, in three rows of four each. If any kings, queens, or jacks show in this layout, remove them and place them on the bottom of the stock. Deal from the top to fill up the layout, moving any additional face cards that turn up to the bottom of the deck, until the layout shows twelve lower cards.

If no face card shows in the original layout, place the first face card turned up in play on the bottom of the deck (for without a face card at bottom the game cannot be won).

With the layout complete (all non-face cards) commence play. Deal cards from the stock on each pair of cards that total eleven. When a face card is dealt, it blocks further play on that pile. The game is won if you succeed in running through the deck, ending with the twelve face cards covering the tableau.

Gaps

Time required: 10 minutes   Chance of winning: 1 in 20 games

Layout. Deal the whole deck in four rows of thirteen cards each (not overlapped). Then discard the aces, creating four gaps.

Play. Into each gap move the card next-higher in suit to the card at the left of the gap. But the sequence ends with king, so that no card may be moved into a gap at the right of a king. Fill each gap at the exreme left of a row with a twospot. To win the game you must get one entire suit on each row, in proper sequence with the two.

Redeal. Continue filling gaps as they are created, until all are blocked by kings. Then gather all the cards not in proper suit and sequence with twos at the left ends of rows. Shuffle them and redeal so as to fill out each row to thirteen, including a gap left just to the right of the cards already in proper sequence. Two such redeals are allowed.

the first such card will be dealt in the space formerly occupied by the $\heartsuit$ J; in the second row, in the space beside the $\spadesuit$ K; in the third row, in the space of the $\spadesuit$ J, and in the bottom row in the space of the $\diamondsuit$ K. Play will then be resumed as before.

Gaps after several plays. Each gap is blocked by a king. Now all cards in the top row at the right of the $\spadesuit$ 3; the entire second row; all cards in the third row to the right of the $\diamondsuit$ 7, and all cards in the bottom row to the right of the $\clubsuit$ 3, should be gathered up, shuffled, and redealt. In the top row,

Bisley

Time required: 5 minutes   Chance of winning: 2 out of 3 games

Foundations. Remove the four aces from the deck and put them in a row at the extreme left. Put the four kings, as they become available, in a row above the aces. Build the aces up in suit, and the kings down in suit. (It does not matter where two foundations of the same suit meet, so long as the entire suit is built on them.)

Tableau. Deal nine cards in a row to the right of the aces, then deal the rest of the deck in three more rows of thirteen cards each, below the first.

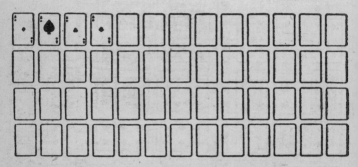

Play. The bottom card of each column is available for play on a foundation or on the bottom card of another column. On bottom cards of the tableau, build in suit either up or down, as you wish. An ace may be built only on a deuce, a king only on a queen. A space made by removing an entire column may not be filled.

Tips. Build on foundations at every opportunity—no hazard is incurred in so doing. The risk comes in building down on a column in which a lower card of the same suit is buried, or up on a column in which a higher card is buried. For example, if a six of spades is built on a five, the nine of spades being in the column, this build obviously cannot be built on a foundation. It will therefore have to be reversed eventually on the seven of spades, to reach the nine. Since such building is often unavoidable, earmark the cards that positively must be saved in the tableau.

Pendulum

Time required: 30 minutes   Chance of winning: 1 in 30 games

Foundations. Remove the four aces from the deck and put them in a column at the right. Build them up in suit by any interval you choose, after examining the tableau. (For example, if you elect to build up by fives, the sequence is: A, 6, J, 3, 8, K, 5, 10, 2, 7, Q, 4, 9.) You may choose to build consecutively (A, 2, 3, etc.). The chosen interval applies to all four foundations.

Tableau. Deal the rest of the deck into six rows of eight cards each (not overlapping).

Pendulum after several plays. The pendulum has just been swung to the left. The building is by threes; note that the ♣ 2 has been built on ♣ 5. The ♣ 6 may now be played on the ♣ 3; then, there being no further plays, the pendulum must be swung back to the right again.

Play. The bottom card of each tableau column is available for play on foundations. In addition it may be built upon the card immediately above it in its column, if that card is of the same suit and next-higher in the selected foundation-sequence. (For example, if the interval is up by fives, the two of hearts may be built on the seven of hearts.) A build of two or more cards at the bottom of a column may be moved from the next card above, if the suit and sequence are correct. A card from the bottom of any column may be built upon either of the two cards at the upper corners of the tableau, suit and sequence being correct.

A space made by removing an entire column may be filled only by a card, if available, that is of last rank called for on the foundations. For example, if the selected interval is up by fives, only nines may go into spaces. It is obligatory to fill a space as soon as possible.

The pendulum. Whenever play comes to a standstill, "swing the pendulum." The first swing must be to the right, and thereafter to left and right alternately. The swing is accomplished by moving the cards in rows that contain gaps (except the top row) toward one side of the tableau, leaving all the gaps on the opposite side. Do not change the order of the cards within the row.

By changing the position of the cards in lower rows, the swing makes new cards available. The pendulum may be swung repeatedly, without limit, until the game is won or becomes blocked.

Five Piles

(Thirteen, Baroness)

Time required: 3 minutes   Chance of winning: 1 in 5 games

Deal a row of five cards. Discard each pair of cards that total thirteen; as, 8 and 5; jack and 2; queen and ace. Discard kings singly. Continue dealing by fives from the stock, one card on each pile, and discard what you can. Only the top card of each pile is available. The last two cards of the deck are spread separately from the tableau and both are available. The game is won if you cast out the whole deck in thirteens.

Calculation

(Broken Intervals)

Time required: 15 minutes   Chance of winning: 1 in 5 games

Foundations. Remove from the deck any ace, two, three, and four. Place them in a row. These foundations are to be built up as follows, regardless of suits:

A, 2, 3, 4, 5, 6, 7, 8, 9, 10, J, Q, K
2, 4, 6, 8, 10, Q, A, 3, 5, 7, 9, J, K
3, 6, 9, Q, 2, 5, 8, J, A, 4, 7, 10, K
4, 8, Q, 3, 7, J, 2, 6, 10, A, 5, 9, K

Calculation Layout—Any two may be played on the ♡ A, any four on the ♣ 2, any six on the ♣ 3 and any eight on the ◇ 4; unplayable cards may be placed in any of the positions indicated by the broken lines.

Play. Turn up cards from the stock one at a time, placing each either on a foundation or on any one of four wastepiles. These piles are best kept spread downward, so that all cards may be seen. Only the top of each pile is available. Cards may be moved up to foundations at any time.

Tips. As a rule, one wastepile has to be earmarked for kings. To lay a king on any lower card is hazardous, since it can be removed only by building up one foundation complete. But when three kings, possibly two, have been laid in the reserve, it may be advisable to use all four piles for lower cards and chance that the remaining kings will not come too soon.

The natural policy is to try to build descending sequences on the wastepiles, corresponding to the foundation sequences. Of course, the cards are rarely so kind as to allow these builds to be extended very far, but a judicious scattering of sequences of two to four cards works wonders.

As a rule, avoid laying a card on a pile that contains another of the same rank, but this rule may well be ignored to maintain a correct sequence.

The finest art revolves around keeping track of how soon or late certain cards may be needed; how deep and with what cards they may be safely covered; whether a card should be played on a foundation or held back to develop another foundation.

Betsy Ross

(Four Kings, Musical Patience, Quadruple Alliance)

Time required: 5 minutes   Chance of winning: 1 in 8 games

Layout. Put in a row any ace, two, three, and four. In a second row below put any two, four, six, and eight. The lower row comprises the foundations, which are to be built up as follows, regardless of suit:

$$2, 3, 4, 5, 6, 7, 8, 9, 10, J, Q, K$$
$$4, 6, 8, 10, Q, A, 3, 5, 7, 9, J, K$$
$$6, 9, Q, 2, 5, 8, J, A, 4, 7, 10, K$$
$$8, Q, 3, 7, J, 2, 6, 10, A, 5, 9, K$$

The function of the top row is merely to remind you of the arithmetic differences by which the foundations are to be built up.

Play. Turn up cards from the stock one at a time, putting each either on a foundation or on a single wastepile. The top of this wastepile is always available.

Redeals. Two redeals are allowed.

Betsy Ross Layout after one play; the ♡ 10 is on top of the waste-pile.

Tips. Spread the wastepile to keep track of all cards. The most vital point is to avoid reversed sequences in the stock. For example, if three cards will turn up in order Q-K-J (regardless of whether they are separated by intervening cards), this is a reversed sequence as regards the first foundation. Some earlier jack will have to be reversed to take off the queen-king, or these cards will have to go on other foundations if the jack below them is earmarked for the first foundation. The ideal is to select for play on the first redeal only those cards, the removal of which will leave all remaining cards arranged in correct sequence for the foundations on which they are to be played.

King's Audience

(Queen's Audience)

Time required: 4 minutes   Chance of winning: 3 out of 4 games

Layout. Deal sixteen cards so as to enclose a rectangular space, the "audience chamber." The surrounding cards are the "antechamber."

Foundations. Whenever a jack and ace of the same suit are

King's Audience after several plays. The ♡ A is under the ♡ J. The ♣ Q and ♣ K have been discarded. The ♡ J may not be played to the foundation row (shown by broken lines) until the ♠ A becomes available.

available at the same time, move them into the audience chamber, the jack on top. The aces are in effect discarded. The jacks are foundations. Build them down in suit to twos.

Play. Turn up cards from the stock one a a time, putting unplayable cards in a single wastepile. The top of the wastepile is always available. All cards in the antechamber are available for play on foundations. Fill spaces from the wastepile, or, if there is no wastepile, from the stock. Whenever a king and queen of the same suit are both available, discard both. There is no redeal.

Carpet

Time required: 4 minutes   Chance of winning: 3 out of 4 games

Layout. Remove the four aces from the deck and put them in two columns, wide apart. Build these foundations up in suit to kings. Between the columns, deal four rows of five cards each, forming a reserve called the "carpet." The layout is as follows:

Play. Turn up cards from the stock one at a time, putting unplayable cards face up in one wastepile. The top of this pile is always available. All cards of the reserve are available. Fill spaces from the wastepile, or, if there is none, from the stock. There is no redeal.

Fortune's Favor

Time required: 5 minutes   Chance of winning: 9 out of 10 games

Foundations. Remove the four aces from the deck and put them in a row. Build them up in suit to kings.

Tableau. Deal two rows of six cards each. On this tableau build down in suit. One card at a time may be moved from the top of a pile to another tableau pile or a foundation. Fill spaces in the tableau from the wastepile, or, if there is none, from the stock.

Play. Turn up cards from the stock one at a time, playing them on foundations or tableau. Put unplayable cards in a single wastepile. The top of this pile is always available.

Dutchess
(Glenwood)

Time required: 10 minutes   Chance of winning: 1 in 10 games

Layout. Deal a reserve of twelve cards, four fans of three cards each. Below the reserve deal four cards in a row for the tableau. Leave room between reserve and tableau for the foundations.

Dutchess Layout—If the $\heartsuit$ 5 is selected as a foundation, it is moved to that row (shown by the broken lines) and the $\diamondsuit$ 5 beside it.

Foundations. Select the top card of any one of the reserve fans for the first foundation, and move it below the reserve. Put the other cards of the same rank, as they become available, in a row with the first. Build the foundations up in suit until each pile contains thirteen cards; the ranking of cards is continuous, ace above king and below the two.

Tableau building. On the tableau, build down in alternate colors. A whole pile must be moved as a unit, when the bottom card of the pile is correct in color and sequence for building on the top card of another pile. Fill tableau spaces from available reserve cards; and, after the reserve is exhausted, from the wastepile.

Play. The top cards of the reserve fans are available for building on foundations and tableau, and for filling tableau spaces.

Turn up cards from the stock one at a time, playing them on foundations or tableau. Put unplayable cards in a single wastepile. The top of this pile is always available.

Redeal. One redeal is allowed.

Gate Layout after the ♡ A has been moved to the foundation row.

Gate

Time required: 8 minutes   Chance of winning: 1 in 10 games

Layout. Deal two columns of five cards each, forming the "posts" (reserve). Between them deal two rows of four cards each, forming the "rails" (tableau).

Foundations. Move the four aces, as they become available, into a row above the "rails." Build these foundations up in suit to kings.

Play. All cards in the rails, and the bottom cards of the posts, are available for play on foundations or tableau. On the rails, build downward in alternate color. Either the top card or the pile as a whole may be lifted up from a rail pile for building on another. Fill spaces in the rails from the posts, and, after the posts are exhausted, from the wastepile. Do not fill spaces in the posts.

Turn up cards from the stock one at a time, playing them on foundations or rails. Put unplayable cards in a single wastepile. The top of this pile is always available.

Tens
(Take Ten)

Time required: 2 minutes   Chance of winning: 1 in 8 games

Deal thirteen cards, in two rows of five and one row of three. Discard pairs of cards that total ten. Discard kings, queens, jacks, and tens only in quartets of the same rank. Fill spaces from the stock. The game is won if you can run through the stock without reaching an impasse.

Fourteen Out
(Fourteen Puzzle, Take Fourteen)

Time required: 5 minutes   Chance of winning: 2 out of 3 games

Lay out the whole deck in twelve piles, face up. Put five cards in each of the first four piles, four cards in each of the rest. Spread the piles toward yourself so that all cards are in sight.

The object of play is to discard the whole layout in pairs of cards that total fourteen; king being 13, queen 12 and jack 11. Only the top card of each pile is available.

Tips. If the two cards totaling fourteen lie in one pile, the upper must be removed as soon as possible, in preference to other available cards of its rank. Take note of all such combinations in the layout, and plan how to break them up; before making any play. Also look for "criss-crosses" between piles. Suppose, for example, that one pile contains 8,5 (reading downward) and another 9,6. It would be fatal to leave these combinations untouched, while discarding the rest of the fives and sixes.

Golf

Time required: 4 minutes   Chance of winning: 1 in 20 games

Layout. Deal five rows of seven cards each, overlapping the cards to form seven piles spread downward. Deal one additional card to start the wastepile.

Golf Layout—The following series of cards can be played off on the wastepile, of which the first card is the ♣ 8; ♠ 7, ♠ 8, ♢ 7, ♡ 6, ♡ 5, ♢ 4; here there are several choices of continuation, but the best is to clear off an ace, thus: ♣ 3, ♣ 4, ♡ 3, ♠ 2, ♣ A. An alternative line would be: ♣ 8, ♢ 7, ♡ 6, ♠ 7, ♠ 8, ♠ 9, ♢ 10. This takes off fewer cards; it leaves the remaining available cards well connected, but so does the first line, which is therefore preferable.

Play. Only the top card of each pile is available. The object is to clear away the whole tableau by building the cards upon the wastepile. Build in sequence, up or down, regardless of suit. The option of direction exists on every play; for example, having put a six on a five, you are not bound to continue up, but may go down with another five. The ranking is not, however, "around the corner." Only a two may be built on an ace, and a king stops the sequence—a queen may not be built on it.

Each time you find no available cards to build, turn up another card from the stock and lay it on the wastepile.

You win the game if you clear off the tableau; failing that, your object is to leave as few cards in it as possible.

Tips. Plan the entire sequence before moving any card from the tableau. With choice between available cards of the same rank, note which of the cards to be uncovered would allow the sequence to be prolonged. With choice between whole sequences, the natural preference is for the longest sequence, but other considerations may supervene, especially at an early stage of the game. It is important, when feasible, to leave available for the next turn a group of cards in sequence rather than unconnected. For example, with a choice of what to uncover in the last play of a sequence, uncover a seven if an eight and a six are exposed elsewhere, rather than an unconnected two, etc.

The most dangerous cards are of course kings. So long as any real prospect of winning remains, reserve queens to take off kings.

TOURNAMENT GOLF is a method of competitive scoring between two players, each playing nine Golf games with his own deck. A player's score for each game is the number of cards left in the tableau. The scores are compared, game by game, and the lower score for each game earns one point for the "hole." A hole may be made in a minus number of strokes —if the player clears off the tableau with cards still left in his stock, he subtracts from his score the number of such cards. The better "medal" score—total of "strokes" for the nine holes —earns three points.

Playing solo, you may consider that in a round of nine holes you beat "par" if your medal score is less than 36.

Monte Carlo Layout—Either ♣ 7 and ♡ 7, or ♡ 7 and ♠ 7 may be discarded; if the ♣ 7, the ♢ J will be moved to the extreme right of the top row, etc.

Monte Carlo

(Weddings, Double and Quits)

Time required: 10 minutes   Chance of winning: 1 in 8 games

Layout. Deal five rows of five cards each.

Play. Discard cards in pairs of the same rank, provided that the two cards of the pair are adjacent in a row, a column, or a diagonal. The removal of a card does not make the two cards beside it "adjacent."

After removing all possible pairs, consolidate the tableau. That is, back up the remaining cards so as to make the rows solid as far as the cards go, from top down. Keep the cards in the same order as they were dealt, reading from left to right and from top row down. That is, push the cards in the highest incomplete row leftward, then fill out the row with cards taken one by one from the left end of the row below. After doing this, deal additional cards from the stock so as to fill it out to twenty-five cards, and resume play. After the stock is exhausted, consolidate the tableau each time all possible plays have been made.

To win the game, you must get the entire deck paired up in the discard.

Tips. If a card can be paired with either of two others, pick the pair that will give more additional plays after consolidation. In the diagram, pair the seven of hearts with the club seven, not the spade seven, so as to bring the red deuces together.

Block Ten

Time required: 1 minute   Chance of winning: 1 in 10 games

Deal nine cards, in three rows of three each. Deal cards from the stock to cover each pair of cards that total ten, and each pair of face cards (kings, queens, jacks) of the same rank. Ignore suits. A tenspot blocks further play on the pile it covers.

The game is won if you succeed in dealing the entire deck upon the layout.

Captive Queens

(Quadrille)

Time required: 4 minutes **Chance of winning: 1 in 2 games**

Play. Turn up cards from the stock one at a time, putting unplayable cards in a single wastepile. The top of this pile is always available.

Captive Queens, showing traditional position of foundations (fives and sixes) and discarded queens. Simpler is to put the foundations in two rows.

Foundations. Put the fives and sixes, as they become available, in a circle. Build the sixes up in suit to jacks; build the fives down in suit to aces, then kings. The queens are thus dead cards. As they turn up, discard them in a pile inside the circle of foundations.

Redeals. Two redeals are allowed.

Double or Quits

Time required: 5 minutes   Chance of winning: 1 in 3 games

Layout. Deal two columns of three cards each, then a card between the columns at the top. These seven cards are the reserve. Deal one card between the columns at the bottom; this is the one and only foundation.

If any kings turn up in the layout, remove them and put them on the bottom of the stock. Deal additional cards to replace them.

Double or Quits Layout—The ♡ 7 is the foundation, the others the reserve.

Play. The object of play is to build the entire deck other than kings on the one foundation, in the following continuous sequence:

A, 2, 4, 8, 3, 6, Q, J, 9, 5, 10, 7, A, 2, etc.

(This is a doubling sequence, with thirteen subtracted each time the result exceeds twelve.)

Suits are ignored in building. Kings are dead cards; a king once placed in the reserve (after adjustment of the layout) must stay there.

Turn up cards from the stock one by one, putting unplayable cards face up in one wastepile.

All seven cards of the reserve are available for play on the foundation. Fill a space in the reserve from the top of the wastepile, or, if there is none, from the stock. The top of the wastepile is also available for play on foundations.

Redeals. Two redeals are allowed.

Nestor

(Matrimony)

Time required: 4 minutes   Chance of winning: 1 in 10 games

Layout. Deal six rows of eight cards each, overlapping the cards to form eight piles spread downward, and leaving a stock of only four cards. Do not put two cards of the same rank in the same pile. If, during the deal, a card turns up that duplicates a card already in that pile, place the duplicate on the bottom of the deck and deal the next card instead.

Play. The top card of each pile is available. Discard available cards in pairs of the same rank, regardless of suits. Each time you reach a block, turn up the top card of the stock and use it if you can, by discarding it with any available card of the same rank. The game is won if you get the whole deck paired up in the discard. (Evidently, the game is lost if you turn a stock card and cannot use it, for by rule it must be discarded. An alternative rule is to turn all four stock cards face up as a reserve, each being available at any time.)

Aces Up

(Idiot's Delight, Firing Squad)

Time required: 2 minutes   Chance of winning: 1 in 10 games

Aces are high, ranking above kings.

Deal a row of four cards. Discard any card that is lower than another card of the same suit. Deal another row of four cards on the (remainder of the) first batch. Play as before. Continue in the same way, dealing the entire deck four at a time on the same four piles. Discard all lower available cards whenever a higher card of the same suit is at the top of another pile. Fill any space, if possible, prior to the next deal, with a card taken from the top of another pile; this may make possible one or more additional plays before you deal again. Aces obviously may be moved only into spaces. The game is won if only the four aces remain at the end, the rest of the deck having been discarded.

Aces Up after several rows have been dealt. Discard the ♡ 8 (lower than ♡ K) and ♣ 8 (lower than ♣ K), then ♡ Q and ♣ 9; move ♣ K and ◇ 9 into the spaces, discard ♡ 4 and ♣ 6; move ♡ K into the space and deal four more cards.

Tips. Use spaces to uncover buried high cards. Do not move aces into spaces automatically—some other snarl may at the moment call more urgently for untangling. But whenever an ace covers another card, leave some other pile that *might* be cleared away by some lucky fall of the cards. Often toward the end it is calculable that no fall of the cards can win. Don't be an ostrich—pick up the cards and start another game.

Bristol

Time required: 5 minutes   Chance of winning: 1 in 3 games

Layout. Deal eight fans of three cards each, forming the tableau. If any kings show, move each to the bottom of its fan. Below the tableau, deal a row of three cards, starting the reserve.

Foundations. Move the aces, as they become available, to a row above the tableau. Build them up to kings, regardless of suit.

Play. Top cards of tableau fans and reserve piles are available to be built on foundations and tableau. On the tableau, build down regardless of suit. One card at a time may be lifted off a fan to be built on the top card of another or on a foundation.

Deal the stock three cards at a time, one on each reserve pile, pausing between deals to play up what you can. Do not fill a space in the reserve except by the next deal. A space in the tableau, by removal of an entire fan, is never filled.

There is no redeal.

Tips. The main problem is to untangle reversed sequences in the tableau—any higher card above a lower. Sometimes tableau-building alone will do the trick, but usually you also have to build up one or two foundations in a hurry to get off a blocking high card. Don't overlook that reversed sequences are just as fatal in the reserve as in the tableau. Save everything you can from being buried in the reserve, especially when some kings are yet to come.

Eight Off

Time required: 15 minutes   Chance of winning: 1 in 2 games

Layout. Deal eight piles of six cards each, spread downward so that all cards are visible. The usual method of dealing is by rows. These forty-eight cards are the tableau. Spread the four remaining cards of the deck separately below the tableau, starting the reserve.

Foundations. Move the aces, as they become available, to a row above the tableau. Build them up in suit to kings.

Play. Top cards of the tableau piles, and all cards of the reserve, are available to be played on foundations, built on the tableau, or moved to the reserve. On top cards of tableau piles, build down in suit. Only one card at a time may be lifted from a tableau pile to be moved elsewhere.

Any available tableau card may be moved to the reserve, with proviso that the reserve may never exceed eight cards. In effect, the reserve cards are held out of play, pending the making of place for them on foundations or in builds on the tableau.

A space in the tableau, made by removing an entire pile, may be filled only by an available king.

Tips. Don't overlook that a tableau space has not the same utility as an opening in the reserve. The latter can be used to consolidate builds; for example, if the ♣ 7 lies on the ♣ 8, both can be moved upon the ♣ 9 by moving the ♣ 7 momentarily to the reserve. But a tableau space cannot be so used, since it may be filled only by a king. Therefore, do not hurry to make a tableau space merely to absorb a king, at the cost of filling up the reserve. Aim rather to release aces and foundation builders while retaining enough reserve spaces to continue manipulation. Be wary of building too many cards above a lower card of the same suit.

Fission

Time required: 8 minutes   Chance of winning: 9 out of 10 games

Layout. Deal seven piles of seven cards each, spread downward so that all cards are visible. The usual method of dealing is by columns. These forty-nine cards are the reserve. Put the last three cards of the deck in a column at the extreme right, forming the tableau.

Play. At the outset, only the top cards of the seven reserve piles are available. After playing off the top card, break the column in the middle by pulling the nearest three cards toward you, so as to form two piles of three; the top of each of these piles is available. When a card is played off a pile of three, the remaining two cards are separated and each becomes a foundation.

The tableau may contain four piles; as originally dealt, it therefore includes one space. A space may be filled at any time by an available card from the reserve. On the tableau cards, available cards from the reserve may be built in suit, regardless of rank. Tableau cards may be moved only to be built on foundations, one card at a time being available at the top of a pile.

Foundations. The "fission" of each reserve column produces four foundation cards. Build all foundations up in suit and sequence, with the sequence of rank continuous (the ace ranking above the king as well as below the two). Available for foundation building are the top cards of reserve and tableau piles. Foundations of the same suit should be consolidated, when they meet, to save room. The game is won if all four suits are gathered together in sequence.

Tips. The paramount consideration is to avoid impasses in tableau building. Obviously if an eight is placed on a seven, the game can never be won. The eight might safely be laid on the six, however, if the seven is in such position in the reserve that it will eventually become a foundation. Take note that the cards destined to become foundations in each column are, from top (bottom of the pile) down: 1st, 2nd, 4th, 5th. Before moving any card from reserve to tableau, trace backward in the suit to locate the foundation that will have to be built up eventually to take it off the tableau. For example, if the $\Diamond$ 2 is in question, find the $\Diamond$ A, $\Diamond$ K, $\Diamond$ Q, and so on, so as to note the first of the series that lies in "foundation position" in its column. Suppose that the $\Diamond$ Q is the first. Then, to lay the $\Diamond$ 2 on the $\Diamond$ A or $\Diamond$ K in the tableau would be fatal, for both of these cards are essential to remove the $\Diamond$ 2.

If the original tableau cards chance to be of different suits, you should usually fill the space by a card of the fourth suit. If two or more of the three dealt are of the same suit, aim first of all to move one or two of them onto foundations, so as to make way for all four suits in the tableau. If, for example, none of the four tableau piles is in hearts, all hearts are for the moment immovable. But sometimes you can make inroads on a blocking suit, without a tableau space available, by uncovering some foundations of that suit.

Strategy

Time required: 5 minutes   Chance of winning: 1 in 5 games

Deal the entire deck, one card at a time. Put the aces, as they turn up, in a foundation row. Put the other forty-eight cards in eight wastepiles, placing each card on any pile you wish.

After the deal, the top of each pile is available. Build up the aces in suit and sequence to kings. The game is won if you succeed in placing the cards so that at the end they will all play off onto the foundations.

Tips. The ideal would be to build descending sequences in suit. But many higher cards are bound to turn up before lower cards of the same suit. The solution is to build partial- and skip-sequences, scattering each suit among the waste-piles in such way as to keep a specific place reserved for each other card of the same suit yet to come. Obviously, you are blocked if you ever lay a card on a pile containing a lower card of the same suit. Similarly, you can block yourself by making criss-crosses between suits. The easiest way to avoid criss-crosses is to build generally down, whatever the suits, and examine the specific situation whenever you must put any higher card on a lower.

One pile must be reserved at the outset for kings, but once a king is down the queen of the same suit can be put on it. With almost the same urgency, a pile must be reserved for queens at the outset, and perhaps a third for jacks—at all events, you must be wary of starting a pile with any card lower than a ten, until forced. As the play progresses, note the specific high cards yet to come and keep some pile available to absorb each (by keeping lower cards of the same suit out of the pile).

Poker Solitaire

(Poker Squares)

Turn up twenty-five cards from the stock, one by one, and place each to best advantage in a tableau of five rows of five cards each. The object is to make as high a total score as possible, in the ten Poker hands formed by the five rows and five columns. Two methods of scoring are prevalent, as follows:

HAND	ENGLISH	AMERICAN
Royal flush	30	100
Straight flush	30	75
Four of a kind	16	50
Full house	10	25
Flush	5	20
Straight	12	15
Three of a kind	6	10
Two pairs	3	5
One pair	1	2

The American system is based on the relative likelihood of the hands in regular Poker. The English system is based on the relative difficulty of forming the hands in Poker Solitaire.

You may consider that you have "won the game" if you total 200 (American) or 70 (English).

Cribbage Solitaire I

Deal six cards face down for your hand, and two face down for the crib. Look at your hand, and lay away two cards to the crib. Turn up the next card of the stock for the starter. Score your hand, then turn up and score your crib.

Put the starter on the bottom of the deck; discard the other eight cards. Deal again and score in the same way. Continue dealing and discarding until only four cards remain in the deck. Turn these up and score them as a hand without a starter.

The object is to make the highest possible total score. By tradition, you are considered to "win the game" if you reach 120.

Cribbage Solitaire II

(Cribbage Squares)

Turn up sixteen cards from the deck, one by one, placing each to best advantage in a tableau of four rows of four cards each. But each card must be put adjacent—horizontally, vertically, or diagonally—to a card already in the tableau.

Turn the seventeenth card for a starter. Score each row and column of the tableau as a Cribbage hand, together with the starter.

The object is to make the highest possible total score. You may consider that you "win the game" if you reach 61.

Cribbage Solitaire III

(Bill Beers)

Deal cards in a row, one at a time (not overlapped), and look for the following combinations in each two or three adjacent cards:

COMBINATION	SCORE
One pair	2
Three of a kind	6
Three of the same suit	3
Three in sequence	3
Three in suit and sequence	6
Two or three that total 15	2

As in Cribbage, ace counts 1, each king, queen, jack and ten counts 10. A sequence is valid even if the cards do not lie in sequential order; for example, 9–7–8 is a scoring combination, as well as 9–8–7.

After scoring any combination, move any one of the cards involved upon any other. Try if possible to make additional scoring combinations by this move. For example, with 9–7–5–6 score the sequence, then move the six upon the seven and then score the fifteen, 9–6.

Each combination must be scored and consolidated at once, before another card is turned from the deck, except that, when a pair shows, a third card may be dealt to see if it becomes a triplet.

The object is to make the highest possible score on running through the entire deck. You may consider that you "win the game" if you reach 61.

Double Jump

Time required: 5 minutes   Chance of winning: 1 in 20 games

Deal cards in one row from left to right. Whenever two cards, separated from each other by two others, are alike in suit or rank, move the one at the left upon the one at the right. To save room, move the cards leftward after every jump (which makes a gap in the row), being careful not to change the order of the cards. One jump may make other jumps possible. You win the game if you reduce the row to three piles after the last card is dealt.

Solitaires
Played with Two Decks

Spider

Time required: 20 minutes   Chance of winning: 1 in 3 games

Layout. Deal fifty-four cards in ten piles, six cards in each of the first four piles, and five cards in each of the rest. The traditional method of dealing is by rows. The top card of each pile should be face up, the rest face down.

Building. The ten piles serve as both tableau and foundations. The top card of each pile is always available. Available cards may be built down, regardless of suit, ending at ace. (A king may not be built on an ace; it can be moved only to a space.)

Any or all of the cards on top of a pile, while they are in the same suit as well as in correct (downward) sequence, may be lifted as a unit to be built elsewhere.

On clearing away all cards above a face-down card, turn it up; it then becomes available. A space made by clearing away an entire pile may be filled by any available card or build.

Discard. The object of play is to assemble thirteen cards of a suit, in correct sequence. Whenever a suit is so assembled on top of a pile, you may lift it off and discard it. The game is won if you discard the whole deck in eight batches. It is not compulsory to discard a suit when able.

Play. Whenever play comes to a standstill, deal another row of ten cards, one upon each pile of the tableau. All spaces must be filled prior to such a deal.

Tips. Prefer "naturals"—builds in suit—where choice offers. Ahead even of this policy, however, is the rule: Make first the builds that you can unmake. For example, if the layout shows two sixes and a five, move the five on a six first, ahead of even a natural build, since the five can be moved later if necessary.

Among builds that are not naturals, start with those of highest rank.

Try to make a space as early as possible. Sometimes this will mean that, having depleted one pile, your prospects are better to continue removing cards from that pile than making natural builds, where choice offers. Use spaces to reshuffle sequences into "naturals" so far as possible, before finally filling them.

Sly Fox

Time required: 15 minutes   Chance of winning: 5 out of 6 games

Foundations. Remove one ace and one king of each suit from the deck. Put them in two columns, at extreme left and right. Build the aces up in suit to kings, and the kings down in suit to aces.

Sly Fox Layout—The outlined cards represent the reserve.

Reserve. Between the foundation columns deal a reserve of twenty cards, four rows of five each. All these cards are available for play on foundations. If any (of the original twenty) is played up, fill the space immediately from the stock.

Play. After play comes to a standstill (and with all spaces filled), turn up additional cards, one at a time, from the stock. Play up what you can (and will) on foundations. Put each unplayable card on any reserve pile you wish. Continue dealing until you have added twenty cards to the reserve (not including cards played on foundations). Only after such addition may you resume playing cards from the reserve to the foundations. Only the top cards of reserve piles are available.

Continue in the same way, adding twenty cards at a time to the reserve before again moving cards out of the reserve. The final deal may, of course, comprise less than twenty cards. Except as to the original deal, spaces in the reserve are not filled at once; but they may be utilized in placing the next batch of twenty cards from the stock. There is no redeal, and no reversal on the foundations (by playing from one foundation pile to another).

Tips. If you lose this game, it will probably be by your own error.

The natural policy is to build the reserve piles in suit and sequence. But do not push this to the point of blocking yourself. For example, if you put a five of spades above a six of spades, don't put the other five over the other six. Two builds of duplicate cards must be made in opposite directions.

Some scattering of the cards of a suit is inevitable, if only to avoid such blocks. Beware of a "criss-cross" between suits. For example, if you put an ace of diamonds over a two of clubs, don't put an ace of clubs over a two of diamonds. This block can be broken in theory—by building one of the kings down to two, while putting nothing on the ace of the same suit—but this theoretic resolution is rarely feasible. Similar criss-crosses among middling cards are less hazardous, but be sure to use their duplicates to untangle them.

One pile of the reserve may well be earmarked for the four aces and kings wanted last on the foundations. By the same token, these end cards can be heaped on a queen or a two, provided only that the king or ace of the same suit is put in a space.

Frog
(Toad)

Time required: 15 minutes   Chance of winning: 1 in 5 games

Reserve. Deal a pile of thirteen cards, holding out any aces that turn up. Square up the pile and put it at the left.

Foundations. Put aces in a row at right of the reserve. If no ace turned up in dealing the reserve, remove one ace from the stock. Put all remaining aces, as they become available, in a row with the first. Build them up to kings, regardless of suits.

Frog Layout—The ♡ 6 tops the reserve pile, the ♣ A has been set out as first foundation; the broken lines indicate the positions of the wastepiles.

Play. Turn up cards from the stock one at a time, putting unplayable cards on any of five wastepiles. You may put each card where you wish, provided that you make no more than five piles. The top card of each wastepile and the top card of the reserve, are always available for play on foundations. There is no redeal.

Tips. You had better reserve one wastepile for kings and queens. On other piles, of course build generally downward, in sequence when able. But of course you will frequently be forced to put a high card on a lower. Then be careful not to mass cards of like rank, subsequently turned, so as to create a block. To imagine an extreme example, suppose that you have covered a six with a jack. Then to add all remaining unplayed sevens to the same pile would be fatal. Of course, it would be bad on principle to mass cards of the same rank in one pile. But the position of all other sixes might be such that to put a single seven on this six-jack pile would be fatal. The ideal is to build two or more piles in complementary segments, so that as soon as a foundation is built up to the necessary height all these segments can be skimmed off, exposing the low cards of the segments below.

Fanny

Time required: 15 minutes   Chance of winning: 1 in 10 games

Follow all the rules of Frog, except: Deal only twelve cards to the reserve. Do not take out any aces to start the foundation row; all aces must be made available during the course of play.

Colorado

Time required: 15 minutes   Chance of winning: 5 out of 6 games

Layout. Deal a tableau of twenty cards, in two rows of ten each.

Colorado Layout—The $\heartsuit$ A and $\clubsuit$ K have been set out as foundations; the other $\heartsuit$ A (in the bottom row) may not be used as a foundation.

Foundations. As they become available, move one ace and one king of each suit into a row above the tableau. Build the aces up in suit to kings, and the kings down in suit to aces.

Play. Turn up cards from the stock one at a time, putting each on a foundation or on the tableau. You may lay the card on any tableau pile without regard to suits or rank; the tableau in effect comprises twenty wastepiles. Each card must be placed before the next is turned.

The top card of each tableau pile is available for play on foundations; it may be moved for no other purpose. A space in the tableau must be filled at once from the stock. It is not permissible to look at the next card from the stock before deciding whether to make a space. There is no redeal.

Constitution

Time required: 20 minutes   Chance of winning: 5 out of 6 games

Layout. Remove from the deck all aces, kings, and queens. Discard the kings and queens. Put the aces in a row for foundations. Below them deal a tableau of thirty-two cards, in four rows of eight each.

Foundations. Build the aces up in suit to jacks.

Tableau. Cards may be moved from the tableau to foundations only from the top row. On the cards in the top row you may build down in alternate colors; available for such building are the top cards in the top row and all cards of the second row. The top card of a build is available for play on a foundation, but not into a space.

A space in any row must be filled at once by moving up a card from the row below—any card from the lower row, not necessarily the one directly under the space. Each space is thus pushed downward until it reaches the bottom row, where it must be filled at once from the stock.

Play. Note that stock cards get into play only through spaces in the tableau; they may not be played directly to foundations. Therefore, if no more spaces can be made at a time when any of the stock remains undealt, the game is lost.

Tips. If the tableau is notably deficient in twos or other low cards, plan at once to accommodate a larger number of cards

Constitution Layout—The outlined cards represent the tableau.

in builds. The way to do this is to get a high card, preferably a jack or ten, into the top row quickly, and bring up "feeders" for this pile from below. In any case, be wary of building on middling-low base cards, say fours to sevens, for such builds do not "pull their weight" in the struggle to make place for new cards.

Generally speaking, move up the lowest card of each row. Certainly, twos, threes and fours must be moved up quickly.

Remember that there are two ways to get a card to a foundation from the second row. One way is to make a space in the first row and move the card up. The other way is to build the card on a first-row pile in passing, as it were. This second way makes a space in the second row but not in the first; it is preferable when the prime consideration is to bring new cards into the tableau (because it is deficient in low cards).

Napoleon at St. Helena

(Forty Thieves, Big Forty, Roosevelt at San Juan)

Time required: 20 minutes   Chance of winning: 1 in 10 games

Layout. Deal a tableau of forty cards, four rows of ten each, overlapping the cards to form piles spread downward.

Napoleon at St. Helena Layout—The ♠ Q may be built on ♠ K, then ♡ 8 on ♡ 9, then ♣ 9 on ♣ 10, ♣ 8 on ♣ 9, etc.

Foundations. Move the eight aces, as they become available, to a row above the tableau. Build them up in suit to kings.

Play. The top cards of tableau piles are available for play on foundations or on each other. Only one card at a time may be moved. On the tableau, build down in suit. A space made by clearing away an entire column may be filled by any available card from the tableau or from the wastepile.

Turn up cards from the stock one at a time, putting unplayable cards in a single wastepile. The top card of this pile is always available for play on foundations or tableau.

Tips. You are entitled to see the next card from the stock before making any decision. Use this privilege.

Drive for a space as soon as possible. This will often involve picking out a pile that has best chance of being cleared away, and refraining from making builds that would usurp the place earmarked for cards in this pile.

Limited

Time required: 20 minutes   Chance of winning: 1 in 5 games

Follow all the rules of Napoleon at St. Helena, except: Deal the tableau in three rows of twelve cards each, to form twelve spread piles. This makes a much better game than Napoleon at St. Helena, since fewer cards are out of play.

Lucas

Time required: 15 minutes   Chance of winning: 1 in 3 games

Follow all the rules of Napoleon at St. Helena, except: Remove the eight aces from the deck and put them in the foundation row. For the tableau, deal three rows of thirteen cards each, to form thirteen spread piles.

Maria

Time required: 20 minutes   Chance of winning: 1 in 8 games

Follow all the rules of Napoleon at St. Helena, except: Deal the tableau in four rows of nine cards each, to form nine spread piles; on the tableau, build down in alternate colors.

Number Ten

Time required: 20 minutes   Chance of winning: 1 in 10 games

Follow all the rules of Napoleon at St. Helena, except: Deal the first two rows of tableau cards face down, the other two face up. On the tops of tableau piles, build down in alternate colors. All cards on top of a pile that are in correct sequence may be lifted as a unit for transfer to another pile.

Rank and File

(Dress Parade)

Time required: 20 minutes   Chance of winning: 1 in 10 games

Follow all the rules of Napoleon at St. Helena, except: Deal the first three rows of the tableau face down, the last face up. On the tops of tableau piles, build down in alternate colors. All cards on top of a pile that are in correct sequence may be lifted as a unit for transfer to another pile.

Indian

Time required: 20 minutes   Chance of winning: 1 in 2 games

Follow all the rules of Napoleon at St. Helena, except: Deal only thirty cards to the tableau, a row of ten face down and then two rows face up, forming spread piles. In tableau-building, a card may be put on the next-higher card of any suit but its own.

Windmill

(Propeller)

Time required: 5 minutes   Chance of winning: 1 in 10 games

Layout. Remove any one ace from the deck and place it in the center of the table, for the first foundation. Deal four "sails" (reserve) of two cards each around the ace, two in column above, two in column below, two in a row on each side.

Foundations. Build the ace up, regardless of suits, until the pile contains fifty-two cards. Sequence is continuous, ace ranking above king and below two.

Move the first four kings (of any suits) that become available into the spaces between the sails. Build these foundations down, regardless of suits, to aces.

The top card of a king-foundation may be transferred to the ace-foundation, that is, one card at an occasion. After such a transfer, the next card put on the ace-foundation must come from elsewhere.

Play. The eight cards of the sails are always available for play on foundations. A space in the sails must be filled at once from the wastepile, or, if there is no wastepile, from the stock.

Turn up cards from the stock one at a time, putting unplayable cards in a single wastepile, the top card of which is always available for play on foundations. There is no redeal.

Tips. Build up the center pile at every opportunity. But don't move cards from the sails to the king-foundations until the wastepile shows a card you need to save. The ideal is to have a wide assortment of ranks in the sails and on king-foundations, for wholesale feeding of the voracious center pile. Don't make spaces in such a hurry that you load down the sails with three or four cards of the same rank.

The usual rule is that the foundation kings themselves may not be reversed onto the ace-foundation. Maybe you will want to eliminate this rule—after you discover that winning the game is not such a cinch as it seems.

Windmill—The other kings will go in the broken lines.

Mount Olympus

Time required: 15 minutes　　　Chance of winning: 5 out of 6 games

Foundations. Remove all the aces and twos from the deck and put them in two rows. Build these foundations up in suit, by twos, as follows:

$$A, 3, 5, 7, 9, J, K$$
$$2, 4, 6, 8, 10, Q$$

Tableau. Deal a row of nine cards below the foundations. All these cards are available for play on foundations, and for building on each other. Build downward in suit, by twos. All the cards on top of a tableau pile that are in correct suit and sequence may be lifted as a unit for transfer to another pile. A space in the tableau made by removing an entire pile must be filled from the stock.

Play. Whenever play comes to a standstill, deal another row of nine cards upon the tableau piles. All spaces must be filled before such a deal. Top cards of the piles are always available for building on foundations or tableau.

Tips. Spread the piles downward in column, so as to see all cards. Watch out for reversed sequences (higher card dealt on a lower, whether or no any cards intervene). Plan the building primarily to resolve such reversals.

The game takes its name from the traditional layout—foundations in one curved row, tableau in pyramidal form below. This layout is too wide for the regulation folding card table, and it does not allow for spreading the tableau piles.

Grand Duchess

Time required: 15 minutes   Chance of winning: 1 in 10 games

Foundations. As they become available, move one ace and one king of each suit to a foundation row. Build the aces in suit up to kings, and the kings down in suit to aces.

Grand Duchess Layout—The bottom row is the tableau, the face-down cards the reserve; the ace and king have been set out as foundations.

Play. Deal a row of four cards to start the tableau, then two cards face down in a pile to start the reserve.

Play up what you can from the tableau to the foundations. Do not fill spaces except by the next deal.

Continue dealing the whole stock in the same way—four cards to the tableau, one on each pile, and two face down to the reserve. Pause after each deal to play what you can, the top card of each tableau pile being available.

After the stock is exhausted, turn over all cards of the reserve and play what you can on foundations. Continue play from the tableau also, if reserve cards make new plays possible.

Redeals. Three redeals are allowed. To form the new stock, pick up the tableau piles in reverse order (each pile on its right-hand neighbor) so that the last-dealt will be at the top of the stock. Then put the unplayed reserve cards on the bottom of the new stock.

In the last redeal, do not give any cards to the reserve: Deal the whole stock to the tableau, four cards at a time.

Parisienne

Time required: 15 minutes   Chance of winning: 1 in 10 games

Follow all the rules of Grand Duchess, except: Remove one ace and one king of each suit from the deck at the outset and put them in the foundation row.

Salic Law

Time required: 15 minutes   Chance of winning: 1 in 3 games

Layout. Remove any one king from the deck and put it at the left. Deal cards upon it, overlapping to form a pile spread downward, until another king turns up. Put the second king at right of the first, and start dealing a new pile on it. Continue in the same way until the whole deck is laid out in piles, which may be of irregular length, upon the eight kings.

During the deal, hold out all aces and queens. Put the aces in a row above the kings. The queens are dead cards; you may discard them in a pile, or place them in a row above the aces.

Foundations. The aces are the foundations. Build them up to jacks, regardless of suits.

Play. The top cards of the tableau piles are available for foundation-building—during the deal as well as after it is completed. A bare king, all cards having been played off it, is the equivalent of a space; any available card may be moved upon the king. But spaces may not be utilized until after the deal is completed.

Salic Law—The foundations, started as aces, have been built up to the levels shown. The outlines represent face-up cards.

Tips. Use the privilege of building on the foundations during the deal to assure that you will be able to make at least one space. Except for this purpose, do not build foundations too high—say beyond four or five.

Faerie Queen

Time required: 15 miutes   Chance of winning: 3 out of 4 games

Follow all the rules of Salic Law except: Do not discard the queens from the deck. Build the foundations up to queens.

After the deal is complete, available cards may be built on the top tableau cards, down regardless of suit. Only one card may be moved at a time.

Intrigue

Time required: 15 minutes   Chance of winning: 1 in 3 games

Layout. Remove any one queen from the deck and put it at the left. Deal cards upon it in a pile of overlapping cards spread downward until another queen turns up. Put the second queen at right of the first, and start dealing a new pile on it. Continue in the same way until the whole deck is laid out in piles, which may be of irregular length, upon the eight queens.

During the deal, hold out all fives and sixes, and put them in two rows above the queens.

Foundations. Build the sixes up to jacks, regardless of suits, and the fives down to aces, then kings, regardless of suits.

Play. The top cards of the tableau piles are available for play on foundations, during the deal as well as after it is completed. If all covering cards are removed from a queen, creating a space, any available card may be moved there.

Laggard Lady

Time required: 15 minutes   Chance of winning: 1 in 4 games

Follow all the rules of Intrigue, except that fives and sixes may not be moved up faster than queens. For example, if a third six turns up when only two queens are in place, it cannot be put in the foundation row but must be laid on the tableau.

Glencoe

Time required: 15 minutes   Chance of winning: 1 in 10 games

Follow all the rules of Intrigue, except: Each five and six must be placed in column above a queen of their own suit; lacking such a queen at the time a foundation card turns up, it must be dealt upon the tableau.

Tournament

Time required: 15 minutes   Chance of winning: 1 in 4 games

Layout. Deal two columns of four cards each, at left and right. These are the "kibitzers" (reserve). If no ace or king shows up, shuffle the deck and start again—without opportunity to make an immediate space in the reserve, the game is hopeless.

Between the kibitzers deal the "dormitzers" (tableau), four rows of six cards each, overlapping the rows to form four-card piles, spread downward.

Tournament Layout—The outlines represent cards dealt face up; the broken lines the positions of foundations as they are set out.

Foundations. Move one ace and one king of each suit, as they become available, to rows above the tableau. These foundations are the "players." Build the aces up in suit to kings, and the kings down in suit to aces.

Play. All cards of the reserve, and the top card of each tableau pile, are available for play on foundations. A space in the reserve may be filled by any available card from the tableau; you may hold a space open as long as you please. A space in the tableau, made by removing an entire pile, must be filled at once with a pile of four cards from the stock.

Whenever play comes to a standstill, deal four more rows on the tableau, thus adding four overlapping cards to each pile. If less than twenty-four cards remain in the stock, deal them as far as they will go.

Reversal. When the two foundations of a suit meet, the top cards being in sequence, any or all cards of one may be reversed upon the other, including the ace or king at bottom.

Redeals. Two redeals are allowed. To form the new stock, pick up the tableau piles (not the reserve) in reverse order, so that the last pile dealt will come to the top of the stock.

Tips. Keep at least one space continuously in the reserve, filling only when you will thereby regain a space. In the early play, be wary of putting "dead" cards in the reserve—those that are wanted last or late on foundations. When foundations have met, it may prove advantageous to hold them intact so that the reversal privilege can later be used to dig down to a vital buried card. Generally speaking, if foundations meet during the first redeal, hold them so until the second redeal, unless opportunity offers to add several cards to both. Toward the end of the first redeal, try to make many reserve spaces—four or more—rather than build at the sacrifice of spaces. (But building two foundations to the meeting point is worth some sacrifice.) In the second redeal, try not to let any soon-wanted cards be buried.

Nivernaise

(Napoleon's Flank)

Time required: 20 minutes   Chance of winning: 1 in 20 games

Follow the rules of Tournament with these exceptions: Deal cards to the tableau in packets, face down, and square them up before turning them over. You may inspect only as many cards at the top of a pile as there are spaces in the reserve. When foundations meet, only one card may be transferred from one to the other.

(The reserve is the "flanks" and the tableau is the "line." Nivernaise is the progenitor of Tournament, but is more tedious and offers less opportunity for skillful planning.)

Virginia Reel

Time required: 20 minutes   Chance of winning: 1 in 4 games

Foundations. Remove from the deck a two, a three, and a four, of different suits. Put them in a column at the left. Move all other twos, three, fours, as the play permits, into rows with these first foundations, all of one rank in one row. You may commence building on a foundation as soon as it is in the row assigned to its rank, but not before. Build up in suit, by threes, as follows:

$$2, 5, 8, J$$
$$3, 6, 9, Q$$
$$4, 7, 10, K$$

Virginia Reel Layout—The ♠ 2, ◇ 3, and ♣ 4 are the original foundations, and other cards of the same rank will be moved into their respective rows. The outlines represent cards dealt face up.

Tableau. Deal twenty-one cards for a tableau, a row of seven to right of each of the first foundations. All of these cards are available for play on foundations, but no card may be moved unless the space can be immediately filled by a two, three or four (whichever is called for by the row). Aces are dead cards, and are discarded from the tableau under this same proviso. The card to fill the space comes from the reserve, or may come from another row of the tableau if there is an available reserve card to fill the space in the other row.

If the tableau contains two or three foundations of different ranks, each outside its proper row, they may be exchanged for each other, but only if the exchange will bring each into its proper row. For example, a two in the three-row and a three in the two-row may exchange places. Similarly, a four in the two-row, a three in the four-row, and a two in the three-row may be shifted to bring each into its own row.

Play. Below the tableau, deal a row of eight cards, forming the reserve. Whenever play comes to a standstill, deal another row of eight cards upon the reserve piles.

Top cards of the reserve piles are always available for play on foundations or (if such top card is a two, three or four) to replace cards moved from the tableau. Do not fill spaces in the reserve except by the ensuing deal of eight cards. Discard aces from the reserve directly after each deal.

There is no redeal.

Tips. The first consideration is to avoid burying foundation cards in the reserve, through inability to make spaces in the tableau. Therefore do not make cyclical shifts in the tableau merely because you can. Such shifts do not make spaces. A foundation in the wrong row may prove of great value, by giving entrance to a foundation card from the reserve. For example, suppose that the three-row is rich in space-making possibilities, while the four-row is not. Then a three in the four-row should be held there until a four is dealt in the reserve.

But a cyclical shift in the tableau may be advisable to save a low card from early burial—a five, six, or seven.

Watch for reversals in reserve piles—a higher card over a lower card of the same suit, wanted on the same foundation. Evidently, such a reversal can be resolved only by the play of the upper card on a foundation in preference to its duplicate. For example, if a heart ten lies over a heart seven (with or without intervening cards), a block will result if this ten is not played up before the other heart ten. Earmark all cards that *must* be first-played of the duplicates; accept all reasonable risk to build up the foundations quickly for this purpose.

There is no point in playing up a face card—jack, queen, or king—until the last card is dealt, except to resolve a reversal. Likewise, there is rarely any point in playing up the first eight, nine, or ten of its suit to appear, if a jack, queen or king of the suit already lies in the reserve, covering no needed card. It is helpful to take note of non-danger formations and piles (e.g., composed wholly of face cards, or containing cards wanted on the same foundation in playable sequence). Concentrate on digging into the incipiently dangerous piles. A major point of judgment is whether to play up the first eight, nine or ten of its suit, when both of the end cards (jack, queen or king of the same suit) are still in the stock.

Despite the great scope for skill in this game, you will frequently encounter a fatal double block or a "criss-cross." Perhaps you will like to play on in the effort to win "half a game": after the last card is dealt, draw out any one buried card, and call the game a half-victory if you then build up all the foundations.

Royal Parade

(Hussars, Three Up, Financier)

Time required: 15 minutes   Chance of winning: 1 in 30 games

This is the same as Virginia Reel, except that no foundations are put in place at the outset. The tableau comprises twenty-four cards, three rows of eight each. The urgency of getting foundations into position so far overrides all other considerations as to destroy nearly all opportunity for skill. The chance of winning the game is slight.

Congress

Time required: 10 minutes   **Chance of winning: 1 in 30 games**

Layout. Deal eight cards in two columns of four each, with room between them for two more columns. These cards form the tableau.

Congress Layout—The broken lines will be filled by aces.

Foundations. Move the eight aces, as they become available, into columns in the center. Build them up in suit to kings.

Play. On the tableau, build down regardless of suit. Only one card at a time may be lifted from the top of a pile, for building on a foundation or on the top of another tableau pile. A space must be filled at once from wastepile or stock.

Turn up cards from the stock one at a time, putting unplayable cards in a single wastepile, the top card of which is always available. There is no redeal.

Tips. Custom allows the player to peek at the next card from the stock before deciding whether to fill a space from stock or wastepile. But the space must be filled before another card is laid on the wastepile. Therefore, do not make spaces by tableau building merely because you can; wait until the wastepile shows a card worth saving. Don't clutter up the tableau with face cards, except as such cards permit space-making builds. Similarly, before moving a card from tableau to foundations, weigh whether it will be more useful if kept in the tableau to save lower cards from burial in the wastepile.

Red and Black

(Rouge et Noir)

Time required: 10 minutes   Chance of winning: 5 out of 6 games

Foundations. Remove the eight aces from the deck and put them in a row. Build them up in alternate colors to kings.

Tableau. Below the aces deal a row of eight cards, forming the tableau. These cards may be built down in alternate colors. One card at a time (the top card) may be lifted from a tableau pile for transfer to foundations or to the top card of another pile. Spaces in the tableau must be filled at once from the wastepile or, if there is none, from the stock.

Play. Turn up cards from the stock one at a time, putting unplayable cards in a single wastepile, the top card of which is always available.

Redeal. One redeal is allowed. (An alternative rule to make the game less easy is: No redeal, but tableau piles may be lifted as units in building.)

Corner Stones

(Four Corners)

Time required: 20 minutes   Chance of winning: 1 in 2 games

Tableau. Deal two columns of six cards each, leaving room between for two columns of foundations; this begins the tableau. Turn the top and bottom cards of each column sidewise; these four cards are the "corner stones." Continue dealing the whole deck in rotation on the twelve piles, pausing to play up what you can to the foundations, under the rules below.

Foundations. As they show up, put one ace and one king of each suit in the center. Lay the ace and king of the same suit in the same row, aligned with a row of the tableau (one of the four inner rows, not the corner stones). Put the aces in one column, the kings in another, and fill these columns in order from top to bottom.

Build the aces up in suit to kings, and the kings down in suit to aces.

Early play. During the deal, play up what you can from the stock (not from cards already laid on the tableau). A card that would otherwise fall on a corner stone may be played on any foundation; but a card that would fall on any other pile may be played only on a foundation in the row of that pile. (The foundation aces and kings may be played from any piles.)

Do not skip any tableau pile in dealing. If a pile is deprived of a card because that card was played to a foundation, deal the next card to it.

Later play. After the whole stock has been dealt, the top card of every tableau pile is available for play on any foundation, also for building on the top card of another pile. On the tableau, build either up or down, regardless of suit. Sequence of rank is continuous, ace being below the two and above the king. You may reverse the direction of builds on the same pile.

When two foundations of the same suit meet, the top cards being in sequence, any or all cards of one may be reversed upon the other, except the ace or king at bottom.

Corner Stones—As aces and kings of other suits become available, the aces will go in the columns below the $\heartsuit$ A, the kings below the $\heartsuit$ K.

Leoni's Own

(Weavers)

Time required: 20 minutes   Chance of winning: 1 in 6 games

Foundations. Remove from the deck one ace and one king of each suit, and put these foundations in two rows. Build the aces up in suit to kings, and the kings down in suit to aces.

Tableau. Deal the rest of the deck in rotation to thirteen piles (as far as it goes) forming the tableau. Construe the piles to be numbered from 1 to 13 (or ace to king). When a card turned from the stock would fall on the pile of its own rank (number), put it instead in a fourteenth pile, face down. The cards so cast out are "exiles." Do not skip any tableau pile in dealing; when a card is exiled, deal the next to the pile that would otherwise have received it.

Play. After the deal is complete, spread the cards of the 13 or king pile. All the cards of this pile, including cards added later, are available for play on foundations. Available also is the top card of every other pile. Play up what you can.

Whenever play comes to a standstill, turn up the top card of the exile pile. If this card is playable on a foundation, it must be so played. If it is not playable, put it under the pile of its own rank, remove the top card of that pile and put it under the pile of its rank, and so on. Continue shifting cards in this way until a playable card is bared on top of a pile. After putting the card just removed under the proper pile, play up the bared card. Make any additional plays thereby opened up.

When an exile card, or any other reached by shifting, is a king, it halts the shifting. Put the king under the 13 pile and turn up the next exile.

Reversal. When two foundations of the same suit meet, the top cards being in sequence, any or all cards of one pile may be reversed on the other, except the ace or king at bottom.

The rule that an exile or a card bared by shifting must be played if possible does not apply to two foundations at the reversible stage. (For the reason that you could circumvent it by reversing some cards on these foundations to preclude the play, later reversing back if you wished.)

Redeals. Two redeals are allowed. To form the new stock, pick up the piles in reverse order (each on its right-hand neighbor) so that pile 13 will be at the top of the new stock; and put the unused exiles at the bottom.

House in the Wood
(Double Fan)

Time required: 20 minutes   Chance of winning: 5 out of 6 games

Layout. Deal out the entire deck in a tableau of fans of three cards each (that is, thirty-four fans of three and one fan of two).

Foundations. Move each ace, as it becomes available, to a foundation row. Build up in suit to kings.

Play. Top cards of the fans are available for play on foundations or on each other. On the tableau, build in suit, up or down as you please. You may reverse direction of builds on the same fan. Sequence of rank is not continuous: only a queen may be built on a king, only a two on an ace. Do not fill a space made by clearing away an entire fan. There is no redeal, and no reversal on foundations.

Tips. Note all fans containing two or more cards of the same suit, and plan first of all to dig out these cards. Remember that upbuilding is a temporary expedient, necessary perhaps to reach buried cards, but that all such builds must eventually be reversed into down-builds to be playable on foundations.

House on the Hill

Time required: 20 minutes   Chance of winning: 5 out of 6 games

Follow all the rules of House in the Wood, except: Foundation cards are one ace and one king of each suit. Build the aces up in suit to kings, and kings down in suit to aces.

Tips. Note the bottom cards of all fans; earmark very high or very low cards to be the bases for extensive builds. When foundations meet, before building them further check that all remaining cards of the suit lie in sequences of right direction to be playable.

Intelligence

Time required: 30 minutes   Chance of winning: 1 in 6 games

Layout. Deal a tableau of fifty-four cards, in eighteen fans of three cards each. When aces turn up in dealing, put them in a foundation row and replace them by other cards.

Foundations. Move all aces, as they become available, to a row. Build them up in suit to kings.

Play. Top cards of the fans are available to be played on foundations or on each other. In the tableau, build in suit, up or down as you please. You may reverse direction on the same pile. A space made by clearing away an entire fan may be filled by a new fan of three cards from the stock. (This is the only way cards from the stock can be brought into play.)

Redeals. Two redeals are allowed. To form the new stock, gather the old stock with the entire tableau and shuffle. As in the original deal, aces (no other cards) may be moved to the foundation row if they turn up in redealing.

The Plot

Time required: 10 minutes   Chance of winning: 1 in 2 games

Layout. Deal a pile of thirteen cards to form the reserve. Since you should see only the top card of this pile, count off the cards face down and square them up before turning them over.

Deal the next card (fourteenth) far to the left; this is the first foundation.

Between foundation and reserve deal three rows of four cards each, forming the tableau.

The Plot Layout—The spaces shown by the broken lines will be filled by sixes.

Foundations. As they become available (and subject to the rule below) move the other seven cards of same rank as the first foundation into two columns, one on each side of the tableau. Build them up regardless of suit, until each pile contains thirteen cards.

No other foundation may be moved into place until the first foundation has been built to the end. As soon as it is complete, all remaining foundations may be moved up from tableau, reserve, wastepile and stock.

Play. The top card of reserve is available to be played on a foundation.

On the tops of tableau piles, build down regardless of suit. Only one card at a time may be moved from the top of a pile to be played on foundations or tableau. No foundation card may be built or built upon in the tableau; such a card turned from the stock before the first foundation is complete must be put on the wastepile.

Until the foundation is complete, a space in the tableau may be filled only by a foundation card from wastepile or stock. Thereafter, a space may be filled by any card from wastepile or stock (never from the tableau or reserve).

Turn up cards from the stock one at a time, playing what you can on tableau and foundations. Put unplayable cards in a single wastepile, the top card of which is available. There is no redeal.

Tips. Clearly, you must build up the first foundation as fast as possible. Play from the reserve at every opportunity—it may contain foundation cards or soon-wanted builders.

The rules do not compel filling a space at once. Take advantage of this latitude. Keep a space open until a vital card turns up from the stock.

Diplomat

Time required: 15 minutes   Chance of winning: 2 out of 3 games

Layout. Deal a tableau in two wings, each wing comprising four rows of four cards each, with the cards overlapping in row. The usual method of dealing is by columns, alternately to each wing.

Diplomat—The outlines represent cards dealt face up; the broken lines will be filled by aces.

Foundations. As they become available, move the eight aces into two columns between the wings. Build them up in suit to kings.

Play. The end card (top of the pile) of each tableau row is available. On the tableau, build down regardless of suit. A space made by clearing away a row may be filled by any available card.

    Turn up cards from the stock one at a time, putting unplayable cards in a single wastepile. The top of this pile is always available for play on foundations or tableau. There is no redeal.

Terrace

(Queen of Italy)

Time required: 15 minutes   Chance of winning: 3 out of 4 games

Layout. Deal eleven cards as a row of overlapping cards, to form the reserve. Below, deal a row of three cards. Having inspected the reserve, choose one of these three cards for the first foundation. Move the two rejected cards (if not of same rank as the chosen card) down to a third row, and deal seven more cards to this row, making nine in all. These nine cards form the tableau.

Terrace Layout—The overlapped row at the top is the reserve; the $\diamondsuit$ 7, $\heartsuit$ J and $\clubsuit$ 6 were dealt next, and the $\clubsuit$ 6 was selected as the first foundation.

Foundations. As they become available, move all other cards of same rank as the first foundation into the row with it. Build the foundations up in alternate colors until each pile contains thirteen cards. The ranking of cards is continuous, ace being above the king and below the two.

Play. The reserve cards are available one at a time, from right (top of the pile) to left. They may be played only on foundations.

Tableau cards may be built on foundations and on each other. On the tableau, build down in alternate colors. Only one card at a time may be moved from the top of a tableau pile. A space made by clearing away a whole pile must be filled at once from the wastepile or stock (never from the reserve or tableau).

Turn up cards from the stock one at a time, putting unplayable cards in a single wastepile. The top card of this pile is always available.

Tips. In choosing the foundation, keep in mind two desiderata: (1) to avoid a rank of which several cards are buried in the reserve; (2) to choose a rank that splits one or more of the reversed sequences in the reserve.

Two cards are in reversed sequence if one wanted later on the same foundation lies over one wanted earlier (whether or no other cards intervene in the pile). For example, suppose the top card is the eight of hearts and the fifth card is the five of clubs. If the chosen foundation-rank is four, the red fours must be built up thus: black five, red six, black seven, red eight. Hence the heart eight and club five lie reversed. However, the selection of any intermediate rank will "split" the two cards and put them in normal order, e.g., if foundations are sixes, the eight will be wanted before the five.

Of course, the candidates for foundation may include no card of the desired rank—or, the reserve may contain more reverses than can be split by any one selection. Reverses must sometimes be resolved by careful play. Earmark one foundation to take off the upper card of each reverse—don't build up foundations willy-nilly and leave one blocked by the reserve.

A block can occur by "criss-cross" among buried cards of the reserve and wastepile. The best insurance against this catastrophe is to build on a foundation only for the benefit of the reserve card available at the moment. Rarely need you depart from this policy—the liberal tableau gives such large opportunity to save from the wastepile cards that will be needed to take off later reserve cards.

Don't build on a singleton tableau card merely because you can. Once it is covered, you cannot make a space there except by building off the whole pile on foundations. Try to start the building on the last-wanted ranks—on sevens, sixes, fives, if the foundations are eights. Save the soon-wanted cards uncovered, so as to make spaces when other soon-wanted cards turn up from the stock. Keep a variety of ranks available.

Once a build has been started, the only reason to refrain from building it at every opportunity is to preserve the chance to make a space.

Blondes and Brunettes

Time required: 15 minutes   Chance of winning: 1 in 6 games

Follow the rules of Terrace except as modified: Deal ten cards to the reserve. Then deal the tableau of nine cards. Deal the next (twentieth) card for the first foundation.

Herring-Bone

Time required: 12 minutes   Chance of winning: 3 out of 4 games

Foundations. As they become available, move the eight jacks into a column. Build them down in suit to aces.

Tableau. Deal six cards in two rows of three each. These cards may be built up in suit. An entire pile is lifted as a unit to be built on the top card of another pile. Fill spaces at once from the wastepile or stock (never from the tableau).

Play. Turn cards up from the stock one at a time, putting unplayable cards in a single wastepile. The top of this pile is always available for play on foundations or tableau.

Kings and queens are dead cards, and may be discarded as opportunity arises. When any jack is in place, one king and one queen of the same suit may be discarded. The custom is to place the discards on either side of the jack, askew and partially under it, so that the column of foundations finally makes a herring-bone pattern.

Redeal. One redeal is allowed.

Tips. You need a large table and a long reach for this traditional layout. It is simpler to put the jacks in a row, with the discards in one row above.

Herring-Bone as it will look when foundations are laid out and kings and queens discarded. The herring-bone effect is in no way essential to the game, and the foundation jacks may be set out in a row, the kings and queens being simply discarded.

Capricieuse

Time required: 20 minutes   Chance of winning: 9 out of 10 games

Foundations. Remove from the deck one ace and one king of each suit and put them in a row. Build the aces up in suit to kings, and the kings down in suit to aces.

Tableau. Deal the rest of the deck into twelve piles, one card at a time to each pile in rotation. (Arrange the piles in any convenient way.)

Capricieuse Layout—The foundations (top row) are set out in advance.

Play. During the deal, play on the foundations any suitable card turned from the stock. (Do not play from cards already laid on the tableau.) Do not skip a pile in dealing; if a pile is deprived of a card because that card was played on a foundation, give it the next card.

After the whole stock is dealt, top cards of the tableau piles are available for building on foundations or on each other. On the tableau build in suit, either down or up. You may reverse direction on the same pile. Sequence of rank is not continuous: only a queen may be built on a king, only a two on an ace.

Redeal. Two redeals are allowed. To form the new stock, pick up the twelve tableau piles in reverse order, so that the last-dealt will be on top.

Precedence

(Order of Precedence)

Time required: 10 minutes   Chance of winning: 1 in 4 games

Foundations. Remove any one king from the deck and put it at the left. As they become available, move any queen, jack, ten, nine, eight, seven, and six into the same row. These foundations must be moved up in the given order; none may be placed until all the higher ones are in place. All foundations in place may be built on freely. Build down regardless of suits, until each pile contains thirteen cards. The ranking of cards is continuous, ace below two and above king.

Play. Turn up cards from the stock one at a time, putting unplayable cards in a single wastepile, the top card of which is always available.

Redeals. Two redeals are allowed.

Odd and Even

Time required: 10 minutes   Chance of winning: 1 in 10 games

Layout. Deal three rows of three cards each, forming the reserve.

Foundations. As they become available, move one ace and one two of each suit into a row above the reserve. Build these foundations up in suit, by twos, as follows:

$$A, 3, 5, 7, 9, J, K, 2, 4, 6, 8, 10, Q$$
$$2, 4, 6, 8, 10, Q, A, 3, 5, 7, 9, J, K$$

Play. All cards of the reserve are available for play on foundations. A space in the reserve must be filled at once from the wastepile, or, if there is none, from the stock.

Turn up cards from the stock one at a time, putting unplayable cards in a single wastepile, the top card of which is always available.

Redeal. One redeal is allowed.

Royal Cotillion

Time required: 15 minutes   Chance of winning: 1 in 5 games

Layout. Deal twelve cards in three rows of four each, forming the left wing of the tableau. Deal sixteen cards in four rows of four, forming the right wing. Leave room between the wings for two additional columns.

Royal Cotillion—The left wing is exhausted card by card, the right wing is replenished as each card is moved. The outlines represent face-up cards.

Foundations. As they become available, move one ace and one two of each suit into the center columns. Build these foundations up in suit, by twos, as in Odd and Even.

Play. In the left wing, only the bottom card of each column is available, and spaces are never filled. In the right wing, all cards are available, and spaces are filled at once from the wastepile, or, if there is none, from the stock.

Turn cards up from the stock one at a time, putting unplayable cards in one wastepile, the top card of which is always available.

Tips. Play from the left wing, whenever you thereby release additional cards. Do not play from the right wing merely because you can; wait to make a space until a card desirable to save turns up.

Gavotte

Time required: 15 minutes   **Chance of winning: 1 in 3 games**

Follow the rules for Royal Cotillion except for the following modifications: Deal sixteen cards in both wings, four rows of four. Choose which wing is to be available *in toto;* in the other, only bottom cards of columns will be available. Choose any two ranks in sequence for your foundations. (Build up in suit, by twos, until each pile contains thirteen cards.)

Alhambra

Time required: 10 minutes   **Chance of winning: 1 in 10 games**

Foundations. Remove from the deck one ace and one king of each suit and put them in a row. Build the aces up in suit to kings, and the kings down in suit to aces.

Alhambra Layout—The foundation aces and kings, in the top row, are set out in advance. The ◇ Q may be built on the ◇ K. If, for example, the top card of the wastepile is ♠ 10, either ♠ J or else ♠ 9 and then ♠ 8 may be built on it.

Reserve. Deal a reserve of thirty-two cards, in eight piles of four cards each. The top card of each pile is available for building on foundations and on the wastepile.

Play. Turn up cards from the stock one at a time, putting unplayable cards in a single wastepile. Cards from the reserve may be built on the wastepile, in suit up or down. Sequence of rank is here continuous, the ace being below the two and above the king. The top card of the wastepile is available for building on foundations.

Redeals. Two redeals are allowed.

Crazy Quilt

(Quilt, Japanese Rug)

Time required: 15 minutes   Chance of winning: 2 out of 3 games

Foundations. Remove one ace and one king of each suit from the deck. Put them wherever you find space after dealing the rest of the layout! Build the aces up in suit to kings, and the kings down in suit to aces.

Reserve. Deal eight rows of eight cards each, turning alternate cards sidewise as shown in the diagram. This is the "quilt" or "carpet." The cards of this reserve become available, for play on foundations or on the wastepile, from the outside in. After the deal, the four cards projecting on each side are available. The removal of any card releases one or two others. The governing rule is: A card is available if it has one of its narrower edges free. (For example, in the diagram, removal of the two of clubs releases the seven of diamonds and three of hearts; play of the diamond seven would then release the five of clubs.)

Play. Turn up cards from the stock one at a time, putting unplayable cards in a single wastepile. The top of this pile is always available for play on foundations. Available tableau cards may be built on the wastepile, in suit either up or down. Sequence of rank is continuous, the ace being below the two and above the king.

Redeal. One redeal is allowed.

Tips. Examine the quilt to see if duplicate cards are both buried remote from the edge. It is usually urgent to dig down to one of these cards as soon as possible. Look for formations that put restrictions on foundation-building. For example, in the diagram, a ten of spades is locked between the four and six of spades. If you should play the duplicates of these three cards on the ace of spades foundation, you would block the game; on the king-foundation, the ten must be played before the six and four. During the first run through the stock, you can do little more than build at every opportunity. But keep track of the direction of your builds, and play on the foundations in a way to avoid blocks.

There is no such thing as an intrinsically "reversed" sequence among adjacent cards (as there is in some kindred games). For example, suppose that you build the five of spades on the four, and the six on the five. This trio is capable of being played off on either a three, going up, or a seven, going down. In the first case you play off the stock; in the second case, off the wastepile.

Obviously, however, you would be blocked if both threes and both sevens were buried lower in the wastepile on the redeal. You may have to earmark certain cards to go on the up foundation rather than the down, and vice versa. Such choice exists up to the time that two foundations in the same suit meet, i.e., have been built up so that the top cards are in sequence. Thereafter, each unplayed card can go on only one of the foundations. The ideal is to resolve all tangles in each suit before building its foundations to the meeting point.

Matrimony

Time required: 15 minutes   Chance of winning: 1 in 30 games

Foundations. Remove one queen and one jack of diamonds from the deck. Put them in a foundation row. As they become available, move the following cards into the same row: both jacks of hearts, and the four black tens. Build all foundations in suit as follows: the queen of diamonds up to jack; the jacks down to queens; the tens down to jacks. The ranking of cards is continuous, ace above king and below two.

Matrimony Layout—The top row are foundations; the outlines represent the reserve (dealt face up).

Reserve. Below the foundation row, deal a reserve of sixteen cards, in two rows of eight each.

Play. The top card of each reserve pile is available for play on foundations. Do not fill spaces in the reserve, except by the ensuing deal. Whenever play comes to a standstill, deal sixteen more cards, one upon each of the reserve piles, and resume play. The final deal will of course comprise only six cards; put them on the first six piles.

After the whole deck has been dealt, and play again comes to a standstill, pick up the sixteenth pile, turn it over to form a new stock, and deal it on the reserve as far as it goes, commencing at the space left by its removal and continuing with piles 1, 2, 3 in sequence. Continue in the same way: each time play is blocked, deal out the next-lower reserve pile, commencing at its own space. If the game becomes blocked after pile 1 has been dealt out, it is lost.

Parallels

Time required: 20 minutes   **Chance of winning: 1 in 3 games**

Foundations. Remove from the deck one ace and one king of each suit. Put them in columns at extreme left and right. Build the aces up in suit to kings, and the kings down in suit to aces.

Parallels Layout—The columns are foundations, set out in advance. There is no play available, so a second row must be dealt to the tableau.

Tableau. Between the foundation columns deal a row of ten cards, to start the tableau.

Play. All cards of the first tableau row are (always) available for play on foundations. Fill spaces at once from the stock.

With play at a standstill, deal a second row of ten cards below the first (not overlapping). All cards of both rows are available. Fill spaces at once from the stock.

Continue in the same way, dealing an additional row of ten cards at the bottom of the tableau whenever play comes to a standstill, observing these rules: Only the top and bottom card of each tableau column is available. The play of an outer card releases the next in the column, that is, a card is available if it has one narrower edge free. When you fill any space, you must fill *all* spaces that exist at that time; you may not pause during the deal to play upon foundations. All spaces must be filled eventually before a new row of ten is dealt, and they must be filled in strict order by rows, left to right, top to bottom. You have option of playing up as many or as few cards as you please to the foundations, before filling spaces.

If there is no space in the tableau, the turn of a card from the stock commits you to deal a new row of ten. In other words, you may not peek at the next card in order to decide whether to make a space.

Reversal. When two foundations of the same suit meet, the top cards being in sequence, any or all cards may be reversed from one pile upon the other, except the ace or king at bottom.

Babette

Time required: 15 minutes   Chance of winning: 1 in 3 games

Layout. Deal a row of eight cards to start the tableau. Continue dealing the tableau by rows of eight cards, keeping the columns aligned.

Foundations. As they become available, move one ace and one king of each suit into a row above the tableau. Build the aces up in suit to kings, and the kings down in suit to aces.

Babette at an advanced stage. The $\heartsuit$ A, $\clubsuit$ A, $\spadesuit$ K, when available, will be moved into the foundation (top) row. The $\heartsuit$ 5, $\clubsuit$ 10, $\spadesuit$ 9 and all cards in the bottom row are available; there is no play for them, so another row of eight cards will be dealt below the bottom row.

Play. After dealing a tableau row, pause and play up what you can to the foundations. A tableau card is available if its lower edge is open, that is, if it is at the bottom of a column or just above a gap in the column. Do not fill spaces at any time.

Redeal. One redeal is allowed. To form the new stock, slide the columns into piles without disturbing the order, and pick up the piles by putting each on its right-hand neighbor so that the one at the right becomes the top of the stock.

Tips. To save room, overlap the cards in column, but keep track of the gaps. Look in each column for cards of the same suit, and look for duplicate cards in different columns. Avoid playing a card from above a gap to a foundation until its duplicate has appeared.

Four Intruders

Time required: 15 minutes   Chance of winning: 3 out of 4 games

Foundations. Remove the eight aces from the deck and put them in a row. Build them up in suit to kings.

Layout. Deal four cards in column at the left, forming the tableau. Below the foundations deal a row of eight cards, starting the reserve.

Four Intruders Layout—The column at the left is the tableau; the broken lines indicate the column in which the four "intruders" will be dealt.

Play. After making all possible plays with the first eight cards of the reserve, deal the rest of the stock, except the last four cards, in rows of eight to the reserve (not overlapping), pausing after each deal to play what you can.

Available reserve cards may be played on foundations or built on the tableau. A reserve card is available if its lower edge is free, that is, if it is at the bottom of a column or just above a gap in the column. Never fill spaces in the reserve.

On the tableau, build down in suit. Move a whole tableau pile as a unit, for building on another pile. Top cards of tableau piles are available for building on foundations. Fill tableau spaces only from the reserve; such spaces must be filled before a new row is dealt to the reserve.

Intruders. The last four cards of the deck are "intruders." Deal them in the column at the right. They are available for play on the foundations or tableau. Fill spaces in this column from the reserve. Once the intruders have been dealt, reserve cards may not be played to the tableau, but only to the intruder column or to foundations.

Triumph

Time required: 15 minutes   Chance of winning: 1 in 2 games

Foundations. Remove the eight aces from the deck and put them in a row. Build them up in suit to kings.

Layout. Deal four cards in column at the left, forming the tableau. Below the foundations deal a row of eight cards, starting the reserve. (The layout is the same as that depicted for Four Intruders, except for the column at the right.)

Early play. After making what plays you can with the first eight cards of the reserve, deal the rest of the stock to the reserve in rows of eight (not overlapping), pausing after each deal to make what plays you can. The bottom card of each reserve column is available for play on foundations. Spaces in the reserve must be filled from the stock, but you may defer filling a space to make other plays. All spaces must be filled before the next row of eight is dealt.

Tableau cards are available for play on foundations, and may be built on each other down in suit. Move a whole tableau pile as a unit. A space in the tableau must be filled at once from the stock. (Note that reserve cards may not be moved into the tableau.)

Final play. After the whole deck is dealt out, you may draw any four cards out of the reserve. The card above each gap thus created becomes available. Drawn cards may be built on the tableau as well as on foundations. Place must be found for each of the four cards so drawn, before another draw is made.

Two such draws, of four cards at a time, are allowed.

Miss Milligan

Time required: 20 minutes   Chance of winning: 1 in 20 games

Layout. Deal the whole deck in rows of eight cards, overlapping the rows to form piles of cards spread downward, and pausing after each deal to play what you can.

Miss Milligan after several plays. The ♠ 2 has been built on the ♠ A in the foundation row.

Foundations. Move the eight aces, as they become available, to a foundation row. Build them up in suit to kings.

Play. The top cards of the tableau piles are available for play on foundations and on each other. On the tableau, build down in alternate colors. All cards at the top of the pile, in correct suit and sequence, may be lifted as a unit to be built elsewhere.

A space made by clearing away an entire pile may be filled only by an available king.

Weaving. After the whole deck is dealt, you may lift up any available card or build from the tableau and set it aside as a reserve, of which all cards are available. After these cards are built back into the layout, on foundations or tableau, you may similarly set aside another available card or batch of available cards. You may continue this "weaving" process until the game is won, or until you find no place for a card set aside.

Blockade

Time required: 15 minutes   **Chance of winning: 3 out of 4 games**

Layout. Deal twelve piles, one row at a time, pausing after each deal of twelve cards to play what you can.

Blockade—The ♠ A and broken lines indicate the foundation row. The ♠ 2 may be built on ♠ A, ♡ 3 on ♡ 4 and ♡ 2 on ♡ 3, ♠ 10 on ♠ J.

Foundations. Move the eight aces, as they become available, to a row above the tableau. Build them up in suit to kings.

Play. The top card of each tableau pile is available for play on foundations, or on the top card of another tableau pile, building down in suit. All cards in correct suit and sequence, at the top of a pile, may be lifted as a unit to be built elsewhere.

A space in the tableau may be filled by any available card or build from the tableau or from the stock. All spaces must be filled before a new row of twelve cards is dealt on the tableau.

Stag Party

Time required: 15 minutes   **Chance of winning: 2 out of 3 games**

Layout. Deal a row of eight cards to start the tableau. Continue dealing the tableau by rows of eight cards, keeping the columns aligned.

Foundations. As they become available, move all fives and sixes to foundation columns on each side of the tableau. Build the sixes up in suit to jacks, and the fives down in suit to aces, then kings.

Play. After dealing a tableau row, pause and play up what you can to the foundations. A tableau card is available if its lower edge is not covered, that is, if it is at the bottom of a column or just above a gap in the column. Do not fill spaces at any time.

Discard all queens as soon as they are dealt, leaving gaps in their places.

Tips. To save room, overlap the cards in the column, but keep track of the gaps.

Gargantua
(Double Klondike)

Time required: 20 minutes   Chance of winning: 1 in 2 games

Layout. Deal forty-five cards in a tableau of nine piles, increasing from one card to nine per pile. Only the top card of each pile should be face up, the remaining cards being dealt face down. The usual method of dealing is by rows.

Gargantua—The ♠ A and broken lines indicate the foundation row.

Foundations. Move the aces, as they become available, to a row above the tableau. Build them up in suit to kings.

Tableau. On the tableau, build down in alternate colors. The top card or all face-up cards may be removed from a pile as a unit to be built elsewhere. On baring a face-down card, turn it up; it then becomes available.

A space made by clearing away an entire pile may be filled only by an available king (with or without a build on it).

Play. Turn up cards from the stock one at a time, putting unplayable cards in a single wastepile, the top card of which is available.

Redeal. One redeal is allowed.

St. Helena

(Napoleon's Favorite, Washington's Favorite)

Time required: 20 minutes   Chance of winning: 9 out of 10 games

Foundations. Remove from the deck one ace and one king of each suit and put them in two rows. Build the aces up in suit to kings, and the kings down in suit to aces.

St. Helena Layout—The kings and aces are foundations, set out in advance. The ♣ Q may be built on the ♣ K, but not ◇ 2 on ◇ A, or ◇ Q on ◇ K. However, the ◇ Q may be built on ♠ J and then on ◇ K; and ◇ 2 on ♣ 3 and then on ◇ A. The ♡ 10 may be built on ♠ J, then ♣ 9, ◇ 8 or ♠ 8, ♠ 7, then the other eight.

Tableau. Deal the rest of the deck into twelve piles around the foundations—a row of four above and below, and a column of two at each side. Deal to the piles one card at a time in clockwise rotation, beginning at the left end of the top row.

Play. Top cards of the tableau piles are available for building on foundations, with this restriction in the original deal: From the top row, cards may be moved only to king-foundations; from the bottom row, to ace-foundations only; from the side columns, to any foundations.

Tableau cards may also be built on each other, up or down regardless of suit. You may reverse direction on the same pile. But sequence of rank is not continuous: only a queen may be built on a king, only a two on an ace. One card at a time may be lifted from the top of a pile for transfer elsewhere.

Redeals. Two redeals are allowed. To form the new stock, pick up the twelve tableau piles in reverse order, the left-hand pile of the top row on its right-hand neighbor, and so on in clockwise rotation, so that the last-dealt will be at the top when the stock is turned face down.

After each redeal, the top card of any pile may be played off to any foundation.

Louis

(St. Louis, Newport)

Time required: 20 minutes   Chance of winning: 9 out of 10 games

Follow all the rules of St. Helena except as modified: After dealing the first twelve cards to the tableau, you may pause and play up what you can to the foundations, filling spaces at once from the stock; but thereafter you must deal out the whole stock before resuming play. In all deals, all top cards of tableau piles are available for play anywhere. Building on the tableau may be up or down, but must be in suit.

Napoleon's Square

Time required: 8 minutes   Chance of winning: 9 out of 10 games

Layout. Deal a tableau of forty-eight cards, in twelve piles of four cards each, arranged around three sides of a square area.

Napoleon's Square Layout—The other aces will go in the broken lines.

The cards may be dealt either one at a time to each pile in rotation, or four at a time.

Foundations. Move the eight aces, as they become available, to the center area. Build them up in suit to kings.

Play. On the tableau, build down in suit. All cards at the top of a pile that are in correct sequence may be lifted as a unit to be built elsewhere. A space made by clearing away an entire pile may be filled by any available card or build, from tableau, wastepile or stock.

Turn up cards from the stock one at a time, putting unplayable cards in a single wastepile, the top card of which is always available. There is no redeal.

Tableau piles may be spread for examination.

Deuces

Time required: 10 minutes   Chance of winning: 1 in 2 games

Foundations. Remove the eight twos from the deck and put them in two rows. Build them up in suit to aces, which rank highest.

Deuces Layout—The eight deuces are foundations, the other cards the tableau. The ♣ 3 may be built on ♣ 2, ♠ 8 on ♠ 9, ◇ 5 on ◇ 6; the ♠ K, if available, could be built on the ♠ A.

Tableau. Deal ten cards around three sides of the foundations —a row of four above, and a column of three on each side.

On the tableau, build down in suit. The top card of a pile is available; or any or all cards in proper sequence at the top may be moved as a unit to be built on the top card of another pile. Fill spaces at once from wastepile or stock (never from tableau).

Play. Turn up cards from the stock one at a time, playing them on foundations or tableau. Put unplayable cards in a single wastepile, the top card of which is available for play to foundations or tableau.

Square

(Pluto)

Time required: 10 minutes   Chance of winning: 1 in 2 games

Follow all the rules for Deuces, except: Do not remove the twos from the deck at the outset; move them into position as they become available. Deal twelve cards for the tableau, putting four cards in each column.

Courtyard

Time required: 10 minutes   Chance of winning: 1 in 2 games

This is the same game as Square, using aces for foundations instead of twos.

British Square

Time required: 8 minutes   Chance of winning: 5 out of 6 games

Layout. Deal a tableau of sixteen cards, in four rows of four each.

Foundations. As they become available, move one ace of each suit to a row above the tableau. Build them up in suit to kings, then add the duplicate kings on them and build down in suit to aces.

Play. On the top cards of tableau piles, build in suit up or down as you please. Once a build is made, it fixes the direction of building for that pile; the direction may not be reversed by later cards. One card at a time may be moved from the top of a tableau pile; thus one pile may be reversed on another. A build on the tableau ends with ace or king.

A space in the tableau may be filled only from wastepile or stock. You may look at the next card from the stock, to decide whether to move it or the top of the wastepile into a space.

Turn up cards from the stock one at a time, putting unplayable cards in a single wastepile, the top card of which is always available. There is no redeal.

Tips. More convenient for examination of the tableau piles is to deal them in two rows of eight cards each, and spread the piles downward as you build them.

Avoid building duplicates in the same direction, unless there is good prospect of later reversing one build. Don't forget that the foundation in each suit goes up first, down later. This means that from the tableau you will have to play off first the down-builds, later the up-builds. Don't move the whole of a down-build to the foundation until you have checked that all remaining cards of the suit in the tableau lie in up-builds.

Crescent

Time required: 20 minutes   Chance of winning: 9 out of 10 games

Foundations. Remove from the deck one ace and one king of each suit and put these foundations in one or two rows. Build the aces up in suit to kings, and the kings down in suit to aces.

Crescent Layout—The aces and kings are foundations, set out in advance. The tableau piles, shown here in traditional crescent form, may more conveniently be set out in rows.

Tableau. Deal the rest of the deck into sixteen piles of six cards each, arranged in a semicircle around the foundations. (This traditional arrangement gives the game its name. The regulation folding card table is too small for it. It is more convenient to deal two straight rows of eight piles each.) The top card of each pile should be dealt face up, the remaining cards face down.

Play. Top cards of the tableau piles are available for play on foundations, and also for building on each other. On the tableau, build in suit, up or down as you please. You may reverse direction on the same pile. Sequence of rank is continuous, ace being below the two and above the king. Only one card at a time may be lifted from a pile to be played elsewhere.

On baring a face-down card, turn it up; it then becomes available. Never fill spaces made by clearing away entire piles.

Reversal. When two foundations of the same suit meet, the top cards being in sequence, any or all cards of one pile may be reversed upon the other, except the ace or king at the bottom.

Shifts. When play comes to a standstill, make a *shift:* move the bottom card of every tableau pile to the top. Three such shifts are allowed. (Note that the shift must be made in every pile, not merely in those piles containing face-down cards. It thus disarranges the builds on piles where the cards are all face up.)

Tips. Only extraordinary bad luck can defeat you, but be careful in building to avoid defeating yourself. Watch the direction of all builds, in order to make all necessary reversals before it is too late. For example, if you have built both fives of clubs on the sixes, one of these pairs must be reversed sooner or later to be playable on a foundation. Yet, you cannot avoid making parallel builds, because the paramount consideration is to get all buried cards into play. The safest general principles are: (1) avoid changing direction of build on a pile unless you see that you can surely split the pile later into two one-way builds; (2) play to a foundation only when compelled in order to get at buried cards, or you can see that the card played is no longer needed in the tableau; (3) hold every pair of foundations at the meeting point until assured that all remaining cards of the suit lie in sequences of the right direction to be playable. The point of the last injunction is that the reversal privilege is invaluable to dissolve a final "snarl" in the builds.

Sultan

(Sultan of Turkey, Emperor of Germany)

Time required: 10 minutes   Chance of winning: 2 out of 3 games

Foundations. Remove the eight kings and one ace of hearts from the deck. Put them in three rows of three, with a heart king in the center and the ace below it. Do not build on the central heart king. On all the other kings, build up in suit to

Sultan Layout—The kings and $\heartsuit$ A are foundations; there is no building on the $\heartsuit$ K in the center.

queens, the ace ranking between king and two. Likewise build the ace of hearts up in suit to the queen.

Reserve. Deal a column of four cards on each side of the foundations, forming the "divan." All cards of the divan are available for play on the foundations. A space must be filled at once from the wastepile, or, if there is no wastepile, from the stock.

Play. Turn up cards from the stock one at a time, putting unplayable cards in a single wastepile. The top of this pile is always available.

Redeals. Two redeals are allowed.

Eighteens

(Ferris Wheel, The Wheel)

Time required: 8 minutes   Chance of winning: 1 in 30 games

Deal three rows of four cards each. From this tableau discard aces singly; discard other cards in groups of four, comprising one face card (king, queen or jack) together with three lower cards that total eighteen. But no group may contain two cards of the same rank (as three sixes, or two sevens and a four). Fill spaces in the tableau at once from the stock. The game is won if you succeed in discarding the whole deck.

Patriarchs

Time required: 8 minutes   Chance of winning: 1 in 20 games

Foundations. Remove one ace and one king of each suit from the deck. Put the aces in a column at the left, the kings in a column at the right. Build the aces up in suit and the kings down in suit. When the top cards of two foundation piles of the same suit are in sequence, any or all the cards of one pile may be reversed upon the other, except for the ace or king at bottom.

Reserve. Between the foundation columns, deal three rows of three cards each, forming the reserve. All cards of the reserve

Patriarchs Layout—The columns of aces and kings are foundations, set out in advance; the cards in the center are the reserve. The ♣ Q may be built on the ♣ K, and the ♠ 2 on the ♠ 2.

are available for play on foundations. Spaces must be filled at once from the wastepile, or, if there is none, from the stock.

Play. Turn up cards from the stock one at a time, putting unplayable cards in a single wastepile. The top card of the wastepile is always available.

Redeal. One redeal is allowed.

Royal Rendezvous

Time required: 20 minutes   Chance of winning: 2 out of 3 games

Layout. Remove from the deck four twos of different suits, also the eight aces. Put four aces of different suits in a row (I) and their duplicates in a row below (II). Add the twos in row II, two at each end. Below these two rows of foundations, deal sixteen cards in a reserve, two rows of eight each.

Royal Rendezvous Layout—The aces and twos are foundations, set out in advance; the outlines represent face-up cards in the reserve.

Foundations. Build the aces of row I up in suit to queens. Build the aces of row II up in suit by twos thus: A, 3, 5, 7, 9, J, K. Build the twos up in suit by twos, as follows: 2, 4, 6, 8, 10, Q.

Play. All cards of the reserve are available for play on foundations. Spaces must be filled at once from the wastepile, or, if there is none, from the stock.

Turn up cards from the stock one at a time, putting unplayable cards in a single wastepile, the top card of which is always available. There is no redeal.

Four of the kings are not built on foundations. Put them in row I to complete the final picture, with the proviso that a king may be so placed only after its duplicate has been built in row II.

Big Ben

(Clock)

Time required: 20 minutes   Chance of winning: 1 in 2 games

Layout. Remove from the deck the following twelve cards: two of clubs, three of hearts, four of spades, five of diamonds, six of clubs, seven of hearts, eight of spades, nine of diamonds, ten of clubs, jack of hearts, queen of spades, and king of diamonds. Arrange them in a circle corresponding to the hours on a clock, with the two of clubs at "nine o'clock" and the rest in sequence clockwise.

Around the rim of the clock deal twelve fans of three cards each. These cards form the tableau.

Foundations. The twelve cards in the circle are foundations. Build each up in suit until the top card of the pile shows the number corresponding to its position on the dial. For example, build the two of clubs up to the nine. Thus, seven more cards are wanted on the two of clubs, three of hearts, four of spades, and five of diamonds, while eight more are wanted on each other foundation.

Tableau. Top cards of tableau fans (one card at a time) may be lifted for building on foundations or on each other. On the tableau, build down in suit, rank being continuous (ace below the two and also above the king).

Each fan must be maintained at a minimum of three cards. The "spaces" in a fan of less than three cards must be filled from the stock (never from wastepile or tableau). They need not be filled immediately; you may continue to build on foundations and tableau, with spaces in abeyance. But if you fill any space, you must fill all spaces that exist at that time. Furthermore, you must fill them in strict rotation. Beginning at "twelve o'clock," restore the first short pile to three cards, then serve the next in rotation clockwise, and so on.

Big Ben Layout—The center circle of cards constitutes the foundations, the outside cards the tableau. The $\heartsuit$ Q may be built on the $\heartsuit$ J; the $\clubsuit$ J on the $\clubsuit$ 10, and the $\heartsuit$ 8 uncovered by the $\clubsuit$ J goes on the $\heartsuit$ 7. The exposed $\diamondsuit$ 6, 7 and 8 may be built on the $\diamondsuit$ 5 in the center, and the $\spadesuit$ 9 on the $\spadesuit$ 8. Additional plays are then possible on both the foundations and the tableau.

Play. Turn up cards from the stock one at a time, putting unplayable cards in a single wastepile. The top of the wastepile is always available for play on foundations, or for building (not filling a space) on the tableau.

Tips. Examine the fans for reversed sequences—a card covering a lower card of the same suit, whether or no other cards intervene. Plan the play to break up such reversals before they become fatal blocks. Do not be hasty in playing to the foundations.

Contradance

(Cotillion)

Time required: 5 minutes   Chance of winning: 1 in 20 games

Foundations. Remove the fives and sixes from the deck and put them in two rows. Build the sixes up in suit to queens, and the fives down in suit to aces, then kings.

Play. Turn up cards from the stock one at a time, putting unplayable cards in a single wastepile. The top card of the wastepile is always available.

Redeal. One redeal is allowed.

Evicting

Time required: 3 minutes   Chance of winning: 1 in 20 games

Deal cards in one row from left to right. Whenever two cards, separated by two others, are alike in suit or rank, discard the intervening cards. Keep the gaps closed up by moving the cards leftward without changing their order. You win the game if you reduce the row to two cards after the last card is dealt.

Solitaires
Played with Stripped Decks;
Four Decks

Xerxes

Time required: 5 minutes   Chance of winning: 1 in 3 games

Deck. Shuffle two decks after discarding all cards from twos to eights inclusive. (That is, use a Pinochle deck of 48 cards, two cards of each rank from nine to ace in each suit.)

Layout. Remove any nine and put it at the left. Below it deal cards in a pile, spread downward, until you turn another nine-spot. Put this to right of the first nine, and start a new pile below it. Continue dealing the entire deck in the same way, putting all nines in a row and starting a new pile below each.

Play. The nines are foundations. Build them up, regardless of suits, to aces. The top card of every tableau pile is available. There is no building on the tableau, only on the foundations. A space made by removing an entire pile may be filled by the top card of any other pile.

Zingara

Time required: 5 minutes   Chance of winning: 1 in 3 games

Deck. Shuffle two decks after discarding all twos, threes, fours, fives, and sixes.

Layout. Remove any seven and put it at the left. Below it start dealing cards in a pile, spread downward. When you turn another seven, put it to the right of the first and start dealing a new pile below it. Deal out the whole deck in the same way, putting all sevens in a row and starting a new pile below each.

Play. The sevens are foundations. Build them up, regardless of suits, to aces.

While dealing the layout, you may put any eight or nine turned from the stock on a foundation. But you may play up no higher card until the deal is complete, and until that time you may not move any card already dealt to the layout.

The deal finished, the top card of every pile is available for play on foundations.

A space made by removing an entire pile may be filled by the top card from any other pile.

Boomerang

Time required: 5 minutes   Chance of winning: 1 in 2 games

Deck. Shuffle two decks together after removing all twos, threes, fours, fives and sixes.

Layout. Deal a tableau of twelve cards, in three rows of four cards each.

Foundations. As they become available, move one seven of each suit into a row above the tableau. Build these foundations in suit as follows: 7, 8, 9, 10, J, Q, K, A, K, Q, J, 10, 9, 8, 7, A.

Play. A single tableau card (not one of a pile) may be built upon another card or pile, up or down in suit. The direction of the first build must be followed in all subsequent builds on the same pile. Owing to the sequence on the foundations, in the tableau an ace may be built only on a king, but either a king or a seven may be built on an ace.

The top cards of all tableau piles are available for play on foundations.

Fill each space in the tableau from the stock, never from another tableau pile. Turn cards up from the stock one at a time (to see the card before deciding how to make a space). Continue play so long as each successive card can be added to the foundations or the tableau, by building or by filling a space. If you turn a card that you are unable to make place for, the game is lost.

Tips. The ideal build starts with a king on an ace. Having started a build, you may as well carry it on so far as you can, since a space can be made there only by playing off the whole pile on a foundation. But there is one exception to this rule, noted below.

Of course it is imperative to avoid building duplicate cards in the same direction. For example, if you have put a jack on a queen, you will create an impasse if you build the duplicate jack on the duplicate queen. Now consider another situation: you have made builds of queen-jack and jack-ten of the same suit. You naturally try to avoid having a common card in two builds in the same direction. But perhaps you could not help

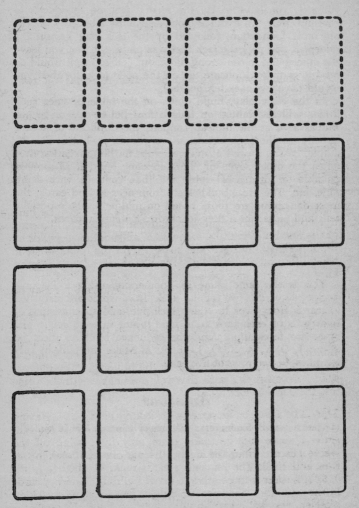

Boomerang Layout—The lower three rows are the tableau. The foundations, one seven of each suit, are placed above, in the spaces indicated by the broken lines, as they become available. The outlines represent face-up cards.

yourself: you have to lay the second jack on the queen to continue play. To avoid a block you must later play off the ten on a foundation, followed by the jack that lies on the queen. If you play the jack that was under the ten, you leave the other build in the wrong direction. (Of course it would be fatal to put the duplicate ten on the open jack, for then you would have two jack-ten builds.)

In the early play, build down on the tableau, since such builds will be wanted on foundations before the up-builds. But as soon as the tableau contains the duplicate of a card already on the foundations, use it for an up-build. For example, having moved a seven of clubs to the foundation row, when the other seven of clubs appears, build it as soon as possible on an ace of clubs, and then continue with eight, nine, etc. The ideal builds start from aces as end cards; the most dangerous are those based on middle cards, especially tens and jacks, since they jeopardize potential spaces.

Sudden Death

This is the same game as Boomerang, using a Pinochle deck of 48 cards (two regular decks from which are discarded all cards from twos to eights inclusive, and so consisting of two cards of each rank from nine to ace in each suit). The nines are foundations, and the sequence built on them is: 9, 10, J, Q, K, A, K, Q, J, 10, 9, A. Make the tableau only ten piles, in two rows of five each.

Amazons

Time required: 5 minutes   Chance of winning: 1 in 10 games

Deck. Discard from the deck all kings, twos, threes, fours, fives and sixes. The remaining cards rank: Q (high), J, 10, 9, 8, 7, A (low).

Layout. Deal a row of four cards to start the reserve.

Foundations. Move the four aces, as they become available, to a row above the reserve. Lay them strictly left to right in the order in which they become available. Build them up in suit to queens.

Play. The top of each reserve pile is available for play only on the foundation immediately above it, except that a queen may be played from any pile. Do not fill spaces except by the ensuing deal. Continue to deal the entire stock upon the reserve, four cards at a time, one on each pile. Pause after each deal to play up what you can.

Redeals. Redeal without limit until the game is won or ends in a block. To form the new stock, gather the reserve piles, each upon its left-hand neighbor; turn over and deal without shuffling.

Even Up

Time required: 2 minutes   Chance of winning: 1 in 3 games

Discard from the deck all face cards—kings, queens and jacks.

Deal cards one at a time in a single overlapping row. Remove and discard any two adjacent cards whose numerical total is an even number. After each discard, close the gap in the row and look to see if there is an added play at the junction. You win the game if you succeed in discarding the entire deck.

Little Lots

Time required: 1 minute   Chance of winning: 1 in 6 games

Deck. Discard from the deck all twos, threes, fours, fives, and sixes.

Layout. Deal the whole deck in eight piles of four cards each, face down.

Play. Turn up the top card of each pile. Discard these cards in pairs of the same rank. Turn up the next card of each pile from which a card is discarded, and continue pairing. When two cards have been removed from any pile, both of the last two may be turned up, and if they are a pair they may be discarded. You win the game if you succeed in discarding the entire deck.

Olga

Time required: 30 minutes   Chance of winning: 3 out of 4 games

Deck. From each of four decks discard all twos, threes, fours, fives, and sixes.

Layout. Deal a tableau of forty-nine cards in seven rows of seven cards each. Lay all the cards in the second, fourth, and sixth rows face down; all others, face up.

Foundations. Move the sixteen aces, as they become available, to two columns on each side of the tableau. Build them up in suit to kings. (Aces are low; next-higher are sevens.)

If in dealing the layout you turn up an ace, or a card playable on a foundation, you may put it there instead of in the tableau. But a card once laid in the tableau may not be moved until the deal is complete. Do not leave any spaces in the tableau because of cards played up to foundations: give the tableau its full quota of forty-nine cards.

Play. All face-up cards in the tableau are available to be built on each other. On the tableau, build down in alternate colors. All cards or any number of cards from the top of a pile may be moved as a unit to be built elsewhere.

Only the bottom available card of each column may be played on foundations. When a face-down card is at the bottom of a column, turn it up; it then becomes available. (Note that the removal of a face-down card in the interior of a column does *not* release the card above the gap.)

A space made by clearing away an entire column may be filled by any available king from tableau or wastepile.

Turn cards up from the stock one at a time, putting unplayable cards in a single wastepile. The top of this pile is always available for play on foundations or tableau.

Tips. Commence by building in the tableau to release all possible cards and also to make a space. Any king blocks access to the cards above it in column; winning the game depends primarily on making enough spaces to get all such kings out

Olga Layout—The second, fourth, and sixth rows of the tableau are dealt face down. Foundation aces are placed at the side, as they become available during the deal and play. The outlines represent face-up cards; the broken lines, the spaces to be occupied by the other aces.

of the way. As a rule, build on foundations not when you can but when you must, e.g., when you must get a blocking king out of the way by foundation-play. Save low cards from being buried in the wastepile; to do so, keep middling-high cards in the tableau until they are no longer needed. Don't overlook that cards higher in a column can often be made playable on foundations by momentary transfer to the bottom row.

Empress of India

Time required: 30 minutes   Chance of winning: 9 out of 10 games

Deck. Shuffle together four complete decks, making 208 cards in all.

Layout. Remove from the deck the eight black queens, the eight red jacks, the eight red kings, and the eight black aces. Put the queens in a pile in the center, with the queen of clubs on top; put the jacks in a circle around this pile. (This part of the layout is purely ornamental. The queen of clubs represents the Empress of India, and the red jacks, her guards. You can save space by discarding these cards entirely.) Put the black aces and red kings in two concentric circles around the jacks.

Deal a tableau of forty-eight cards, in four rows of twelve cards each. All cards of the upper two rows, the "army," must be red, and all of the lower two rows, the "navy," black. In dealing, put each card in the section of its own color, and if any excess of either color is turned up put these cards in the wastepile.

Foundations. Build the black aces up in suit to kings and the red kings down in suit to aces. Owing to the discard of the black queens and red jacks, the black foundations will skip from jacks to kings, and the red will skip from queens to tens

Corresponding cards

BLACK:	A	2	3	4	5	6	7	8	9	10	J	K
RED:	K	Q	10	9	8	7	6	5	4	3	2	A

Empress of India Layout

This layout has been consolidated to take less room than the traditional layout described in the text. The ornamental part is omitted. Foundation kings and aces are turned sidewise. The upper two rows of the tableau, all red cards, are the "army"; the lower two rows, all black, are the "navy." At bottom is one wastepile of each color. The outlines represent face-up cards.

Play. Cards may be moved to the foundations only from the tableau, and then only in couples of corresponding cards, one red and one black. The couples are shown by the columns of the foregoing table—a black two and a red queen, etc. Fill a space in the tableau at once from the top of the wastepile of same color (see below).

Spaces may be made in the tableau by building any card, red or black, on its corresponding card of opposite color (as shown in the table). Later the build may be picked up and distributed upon two foundations.

Turn up cards from the stock one at a time, putting them in two wastepiles, one red and one black. These cards may be brought into play only through spaces in the "army" and "navy."

Knockout

(Hope Deferred)

Time required: 3 minutes   Chance of winning: 1 in 3 games

Discard from the deck all twos, threes, fours, fives, and sixes.

Deal a row of three cards. If any are clubs, discard them and fill the spaces from the stock. Continue dealing three cards at a time, one on each pile. After each deal, discard any clubs that show. Fill a space (removal of an entire pile) at once with one card from the stock. Cease play after you have made five complete deals of three (fifteen cards plus any dealt to fill spaces).

Gather all the cards exclusive of discarded clubs, shuffle them, and commence dealing again in the same way. Two such redeals are allowed.

To win the game you must get all eight clubs into the discard pile.

Russian Bank

(Crapette)

Russian Bank is a game for two players, resembling double solitaire in that the object of play is to build on foundations. But it differs from other double solitaires in that the contestants play alternately, instead of simultaneously. Furthermore, the play is governed by strict rules of procedure, violation of which ends the player's turn.

Decks. Each player is provided with a regulation deck of 52 cards, which rank as in other solitaires (ace low).

Preliminaries. One deck is spread face down, and each player draws a card. The lower card gives the right to play first. Each player then shuffles the deck to be used by his opponent.

Layout. Each player deals a pile of twelve cards face down at his right, forming his *reserve;* then deals a column of four cards face up, above the reserve. The two columns so dealt, the *tableau,* are common property.

Foundations. Every ace, as it becomes available, must be moved to the *center.* Aces are built up in suit to kings.

Tableau building. Tableau cards may be built down in alternate colors. Available for this purpose are other tableau cards (only the top card of a pile), the top of the reserve, and a card turned up from the stock. Only one card at a time may be lifted from a tableau pile for building elsewhere. A space may be filled from the tableau or from the reserve (when the reserve is exhausted, from the stock).

Commencing play. At his first turn, the player must begin by making all possible plays from tableau to center (foundations). Then he must turn the top card of his reserve face up. At all later turns, the player is entitled to turn up the top of his reserve (if it chances to be face down), before making any play.

The reserve. The top card of the reserve must be played to the center ahead of any playable card in the tableau. But in

building and filling spaces on the tableau, other tableau cards or the reserve card may be used in any order. (Of course, spaces are held open to facilitate releasing desired cards, but eventually the player gets rid of as many reserve cards as he can into the tableau.)

The stock. When no play to the center is possible, and his reserve card cannot be put into the tableau, the player may turn up the top card of his stock. (The proviso means that all tableau spaces must be filled prior to the turn from stock, but it does not mean that the player is bound to make all possible tableau builds and fill all possible spaces.)

The stock card is available for play on foundations or tableau. If it is so played, the next stock card may be turned up under the same rule—that no play can be made to the center and the reserve card is immovable. The player's turn continues so long as he can play the cards he turns from his stock. When he reaches an unplayable card, it must be laid face up on his *wastepile,* and his turn ends. (The act of laying a card on his wastepile ends his turn, even though he instantly realizes that the card could have been played.)

Wastepile. Cards on the wastepile may *never* be removed for any purpose. But after his stock is exhausted, the player turns over his wastepile to form a new stock.

Loading. A player may *load* his opponent's reserve card and also his wastepile, by building on them in suit, up or down. Available for this purpose are cards from the tableau, his own reserve and stock. If the opponent has failed to turn up the top card of his reserve when his turn ends, he may be required to turn it up at any time.

Procedure. To recapitulate the rules of procedure:

1. A play to the center takes precedence over all else, except the act (on a later turn) of turning up the top card of the reserve.

Russian Bank Layout—At the player's right is his reserve; at left, his stock. Between the two he will place his wastepile. The columns on each side are the tableau. Broken lines in the center show where the aces will go.

2. In play to the center, the reserve takes precedence over tableau and stock.

3. The stock card may not be turned up so long as the reserve card is playable. (It is playable if a space in fact exists in the tableau, but is not deemed playable because a space could be made by manipulation.)

4. Except as above, there is no order of precedence among plays from reserve to tableau, builds and space-making in the tableau, loading the opponent.

5. A stock card is playable only if it can be laid on a tableau or center pile, or loaded on the opponent's reserve or wastepile. It is not playable by reason of the fact that further manipulation of the tableau could make place for it on tableau or center. An unplayable stock card must be laid on the wastepile; it is no longer available, and the player's turn ends.

Stops. If a player makes an error of procedure under the foregoing rules, his opponent may cry "Stop!" Play must cease on any such call. If the error is thereupon proved, the player's turn ends.

In some circles a false call of "Stop!" is penalized: one card face down is transferred from the player's reserve to the offender's reserve.

Local practices vary as to when an error is deemed to have been made, and when deemed to have been condoned. The strictest rule is that it is an error to touch any card, except in saying "I arrange," when another should be played ahead of it. It is fairly generally agreed that a player may not be stopped if he is permitted to complete another play after his erroneous play.

Scoring. The first player to get rid of his entire reserve and stock into the tableau and foundations wins the game. He scores 30 for winning, plus 1 point for each card left in the opponent's stock and wastepile, and 2 points for each card left in his reserve; including all cards that have been loaded on these piles.

PUZZLES PUZZLES

☐	13535	Bantam Crossword Puzzle Book #2 Luzzatto	99¢
☐	13536	Bantam Crossword Puzzle Book #3 Luzzatto	99¢
☐	13537	Bantam Crossword Puzzle Book #4 Luzzatto	99¢
☐	13538	Bantam Crossword Puzzle Book #5 Luzzatto	99¢
☐	13216	The Bantam Crossword Dictionary Fried	$2.50
☐	14932	The Backgammon Book Jacoby & Crawford	$3.95
☐	10451	The Bantam Trivia Quiz Book Saltz	$1.50
☐	13241	The Bantam Trivia Quiz Book #2 Saltz	$1.95
☐	14487	Complete Book of Solitaire & Patience Games Moorehead	$2.25
☐	14302	Winning Contract Bridge Book Kaplan	$2.75
☐	13053	Bobby Fischer Teaches Chess Fischer, Marguiles & Mosenfelder	$2.95
☐	11811	The TV Guide Quiz Book Goldstein & Goldstein	$1.95

CROSSWORDS

JULIUS ONEADAY HIDE&SEEK

LUZZATTO WORD+CROSS PU

Buy them at your local bookstore or use this handy coupon for ordering:

Bantam Books, Inc., Dept. PZ, 414 East Golf Road, Des Plaines, Ill. 60016

Please send me the books I have checked above. I am enclosing $_____ (please add $1.00 to cover postage and handling). Send check or money order —no cash or C.O.D.'s please.

Mr/Mrs/Miss_____

Address_____

City_____ State/Zip_____

PZ—7/80

Please allow four to six weeks for delivery. This offer expires 1/81.

Bantam Book Catalog

Here's your up-to-the-minute listing of over 1,400 titles by your favorite authors.

This illustrated, large format catalog gives a description of each title. For your convenience, it is divided into categories in fiction and non-fiction—gothics, science fiction, westerns, mysteries, cookbooks, mysticism and occult, biographies, history, family living, health, psychology, art.

So don't delay—take advantage of this special opportunity to increase your reading pleasure.

Just send us your name and address and 50¢ (to help defray postage and handling costs).